Paddling South Carolina

Paddling South Carolina

A Guide to Palmetto State River Trails

• REVISED EDITION •

GENE ABLE and **JACK HORAN**

SANDLAPPER PUBLISHING CO., INC.

REVISED EDITION
© 2001 Gene Able and Jack Horan

ISBN 10: 0-87844-161-1
ISBN 13: 978-0-87844-161-7

Second printing, 2005

First edition published 1986
© 1986 Gene Able and Jack Horan
ISBN 0-87844-101-8

Published by Sandlapper Publishing Co., Inc.
        Orangeburg, South Carolina 29115 USA

Maps by Tony Mitchell

Chattooga River rapids maps adapted from *North Georgia Canoeing*
by Bob Sehlinger and Don Otey

Front cover photo: Horseshoe Creek, at tributary of the Ashepoo River
by Jack Horan

Manufactured in the United States of America

Library of Congress Cataloging-in-Publication Data

Able, Gene.
    Paddling South Carolina : a guide to Palmetto State river trails / by
Gene Able and Jack Horan ; [maps by Tony Mitchell].—Rev. ed.
        p. cm.
    Includes bibliographical references and index.
    ISBN 0-87844-161-1
        1. Rivers—South Carolina—Recreational use—Guidebooks. 2.
Boats and boating—South Carolina—Guidebooks. I. Horan, Jack. II.
Title.

GV776:S6 A24 2001
797.1'22'29757—dc21
                                                    2001034167

Dedication

This book is dedicated to Gene Able, writer, author,
and outdoorsman, who passed away on May 28, 2001.

Acknowledgements

The authors would like to express appreciation to the many people who contributed to this book. Samuel E. Baker of the National Weather Service in Columbia, Mark Dillard of the Attorney General's office, John Gissendanner of the U.S. Geological Survey in Columbia, and Jim Sorrow of the S.C. Department of Natural Resources provided information on hydrology, legal rights, mileage, and wildlife. Bill Craig of the U.S. Forest Service in Columbia, John Fairley of Charlotte, and Ron Hall of Marion reviewed certain chapters for accuracy and detail as did park rangers at the Congaree National Park on the streams that course through the Congaree Swamp. Frank Kiesler shared his expertise on the whimsical nature of the lower Saluda.

In addition, of the many friends who accompanied us on our river suveys, we'd like to extend a special thanks to those who made several trips: Perry and Bonnie Baker, Beverly Baskin, Maurice and Motty Blackburn, Bob Dennis, Zenie Ingram, Maureen Maloney, David K. Phillips, Don Sturkey, John Vaughan, Harold Warren, Jeffrey West, Chip and Martha Whitfield, Mike Boone, Charlene Coleman, Kathie Livingston, Bill Marshall, Richard Mikell, Dave and Dianne Mullis, Lee and Anne Olson, and Alice Riddle.

Maps

The maps in this book are designed for access information. They are not charted to scale; however, the inset with each map indicates the distance from one major access point to another.

● This symbol designates a landing or ramp.

▲ This symbol designates throw-in, pull-out access points.

CAUTION

There is always the possibility of danger or injury while participating in outdoor activity. The material in this book is provided as assistance in planning outings on South Carolina's waterways. The authors have made every attempt to provide helpful, accurate information. No guidebook is a substitute for common sense, however, so the adventurer should be as prepared as possible for the unexpected before leaving home. The authors and publisher take no responsibility for accidents or injuries sustained by those using this book as a guide to paddling the river trails of South Carolina.

Contents

PART II

PART III

Part I

Four Holes Swamp

Introduction

Few states have as splendid a diversity of rivers and streams as does South Carolina.

From the crashing, glass-clear waters of the Chattooga River in the northwestern mountains to the tranquil blackwater swamps of the Lowcountry, South Carolina contains hundreds of miles of relatively unspoiled, free-flowing rivers.

Canoeists and kayakers can choose from among a wide array of downriver paddling trips within the 200-mile-wide bounds of the state: quiet day floats on the cypress-lined Little Pee Dee; overnight excursions through the Sumter National Forest on the swift-moving Enoree or Tyger; whitewater playing in the rock-strewn rapids of the Saluda within sight of downtown Columbia.

South Carolina, with its mountains-to-sea geography, its warm and humid climate and its largely rural landscape, can be called a paddler's paradise.

The state's streams and rivers, spread like tiny arteries over its 31,055 square miles, add up to about 30,000 miles—a significant amount navigable by paddle craft. Moderate temperatures and ample rainfall allow canoeists to dip their paddles year-round—except during the winter months in the mountains when the river environs become too frigid, and perhaps during the peak of summer when Lowcountry swamps become unbearably sultry.

For naturalists, sportsmen, and sportswomen, South Carolina rivers offer a world whose rhythm and pace is governed by the seasonal rise and fall of water. These enchanting corridors convey one to the hushed and secluded domain of the wood duck, the river otter, and the redbreast sunfish. The human visitor passing through these lush green—or in winter, stark and gray—enclaves can glimpse nature's handiwork hidden from the land-bound. A twist of the paddle blade can reveal the purple garlands of wild wisteria, the pink blush of mountain laurel, and the ivory flower of the water lily.

From the highway bridge, all rivers may look the same. Experienced paddlers know each river has its own distinctive feel, however subtle. It may be discerned by the arrangement of rocks in a rapid, by the tilt of the land, or by the mix of vegetation along the shore. Or it may be sensed by the nudge of a crosscurrent, by a slight shift in the hull, or by the tension on a paddle shaft.

In putting together this book, we tried to capture the natural and historical character of each river as well as to provide basic information essential to a successful trip.

The rivers described in the book represent the best in South Carolina for canoeing and kayaking. All told, they make up a system of trails that cover more than 1,300 miles. We have paddled each trail at least once; some sections have been floated two or three times.

By our definition, a river trail is a free-flowing section that gives the paddler a sense of adventure and intimacy with the river and its environment. It may be the entire length of a river (the Chattooga), the most navigable portions (the Edisto), or a comparatively short span of a much larger river (a free-flowing section of the Catawba).

We have not included the larger rivers of the state in our trail system. We recognize that many people like to ply these rivers, whether in canoes or in motor boats. To satisfy this need, we are providing brief descriptions of these rivers in a separate section. We list the major access points and mileages between landmarks, although we haven't personally explored these waterways.

We hope this book will enable readers to enjoy not only the thrill and delight of paddling in South Carolina waters but also help them understand and appreciate the natural beauty and historic charm that remains preserved in them.

Gene Able
Jack Horan

South Carolina Overview

Geography and Climate

South Carolina is made up of three general physiographic regions: the Blue Ridge or mountains, the Piedmont or Midlands, and the Coastal Plain or Lowcountry. The Lowcountry makes up two thirds of the state.

These regions not only represent differing climates, land forms, and vegetation but they also determine the character of the rivers that flow through them.

Here is a brief description of each region and how it influences the rivers and their watersheds:

Mountains. Steep terrain, some stream gradients greater than 250 feet per mile. The steep terrain lets much of the rain and snowfall run off rapidly. Groundwater also feeds mountain rivers, providing a minimum steady year-round flow—these are the whitewater rivers of the state.

Piedmont. Rolling hills that begin at 1,000 feet above sea level, the base of the mountains, and end at 400 feet, the Fall Line, so named because of the waterfalls and shoals found at that elevation. Stream gradients range from 60 feet per mile to about 5 feet. Piedmont stream flows depend on rainfall. These waters are usually tinted red from the Piedmont's clay soils.

Lowcountry. Moderately sloped to flat streambeds that begin at the 400-foot mark. Stream gradients run from 20 to 3.5 feet per mile. The highly permeable soils absorb rainfall and retard runoff to the rivers. As a result, stream flows rise and fall gradually. These are the blackwater rivers, so named because of the tea-colored water caused by decaying vegetation.

The state's rivers fall into four main basins, some of which cross the physiographic regions. The basins are the Ashley-Combahee-Edisto (which includes those three rivers plus the Coosawhatchie), the Pee Dee (which includes the Black, Little Pee Dee, Lynches, Great Pee Dee, and Waccamaw), the Santee (which includes the Broad, Catawba-Wateree, Congaree, Saluda, and Santee), and the Savannah (which includes the Chattooga, Chauga, and Savannah).

Rivers rise to their highest levels during the early spring months of March and April and often reach flood stages. They slowly fall during the summer, though periodic thunderstorms may boost them for several days, and reach their lowest points in the fall months of September, October, and November. As autumn and winter storms replenish the watersheds, the rivers rise and the cycle begins anew.

The ideal times for canoeing and kayaking are in late spring and summer on mountain rivers; late spring, summer, and fall in the Piedmont; and most any time other than the dead of summer in the Lowcountry.

Like other southeastern states, South Carolina has a climate that can be described as mild to subtropical. Piedmont and Lowcountry summers are long and humid, often reaching 100 degrees Fahrenheit several days a year.

Winters in the mountains can be equally harsh in the extreme, dropping to zero degrees on occasion. The annual average temperature is about 61 degrees, ranging from 55.2 degrees at Caesars Head in the mountains to 66.2 degrees at Beaufort on the coast.

Rainfall is ample. Most rivers are floatable year-round. The state gets about 48 inches a year of rain and snow, although snowfall depths may only amount to an inch or two per winter. Severe droughts occur about once every 15 years, lesser droughts about once every 7 years.

Wildlife

South Carolina's rivers and adjoining wetlands and swamp forests nurture a cornucopia of wildlife, ranging from the graceful great blue heron that forages for fish along the edge of rivers to the beaver that has returned to Piedmont and Lowcountry waters. Canoeists floating quietly on most any river are likely to see a variety of mammals, birds, and reptiles in all but the coldest months.

Wild creatures accent a trip nicely. Consider what John Lawson, the British explorer and natural historian, encountered in South Carolina during his trek in 1701. "When we were all asleep, in the Beginning of the Night, we were awaken'd with the dismall'st and most hideous Noise that ever pierc'd my Ears . . . ." he recounted in *A New Voyage to Carolina*. "Our Indian Pilot (who knew these Parts very well) acquainted us, that it was customary to hear such Musick along that Swamp-side, there being endless Numbers of Panthers, Tygers, and Wolves, and other Beasts of Prey. . . ."

Now, more than three centuries later, no such animals haunt the Santee's swamp. Predators like the panther and the wolf have been extirpated since the 1800s. But many swamps and forests remain intact to some degree, providing refuges for wildlife despite the onslaughts of land clearing, development, and pollution.

Canoes offer an advantage for wildlife observation due to their silence and maneuverability. The best approach combines patience and stealth. The ideal times of the day for seeing wildlife are early morning and dusk, when most animals are active.

Aquatic creatures seem to be most active during the spring, when they breed and nest. That's also the time of the highest water levels, however, which allows animals to move back into flooded swamps and sloughs where they can hide.

Still, the days of early spring and summer will be the most rewarding for wildlife sightings.

Mammals and Birds

Here's a description of some of the most common animals and birds canoeists are likely to see.

White-tailed deer. Abundant all over the state. In fact, South Carolina has an estimated one million, one deer for every four people. The tawny or reddish coats and white tails of these animals may be hard to spot through thick foliage beside a river. But, when spooked, the sharp crack of their hooves on the forest floor leaves no doubt as to their presence.

Otter. Remarkably, these playful animals are widely distributed and are most plentiful in the Lowcountry rivers. They have small ears and light tan or brown fur and are about three feet long.

Beaver. Once nearly extinct, the beaver has made a comeback over the past five decades. They are now found statewide. Look for chiseled trees and stripped saplings along the banks of rivers, such as the Little Pee Dee and the Lumber, as evidence of these nocturnal rodents.

Red-Shouldered hawk. If you see a hawk flying overhead on a river trip, chances are it's the red-shouldered hawk. Though their reddish shoulders and narrowly banded tail may be hard to make out, these hawks can be identified by their piercing "kee-yeer, kee-yeer" cry.

Barred owl. At night, the dominant sound in Lowcountry river swamps, above the chirring of crickets, is that of the barred owl. This large, brown-and-white owl makes a series of hoots that sound as if someone is saying, "Who cooks for you? Who cooks for you? Aww."

Great blue heron. This heron is easy to recognize because of its reed-thin body, its slate-blue feathers, and its four-foot wingspan. Particularly abundant on Piedmont rivers, its hoarse call resembles the swinging of a gate with a rusty hinge.

Osprey. Also called a fish eagle, the osprey hunts the open waters. It is most common along the coast but can be seen on upland rivers such as the Catawba. The osprey is nearly as big as the bald eagle and has similar markings. Viewed from underneath, the osprey shows a brown-and-white tail while the bald eagle displays a white tail. The osprey makes a loud chirping sound.

Bald eagle. The national bird rebounded so well in South Carolina and elsewhere in the contiguous 48 states that it was taken off the federal endangered species list in 1999. In 1977 biologists counted 13 nesting pairs along the South Carolina

photos courtesy of *South Carolina Wildlife* Magazine

Eastern black bear cub   Prothonotary warbler

coast. By 2001, that number had risen to 147 nesting pairs. Bald eagles now nest in 31 of the state's 46 counties.

American egret. This all-white heron with a yellow bill and black legs can be found in both fresh and saltwater marshes, yet it also ranges inland. It makes a deep croaking sound.

Prothonotary warbler. No trip down a swamp river like Four Holes Swamp or Wambaw Creek is complete without seeing this colorful warbler. The male flashes its brilliant gold chest as it flits from tree to tree. Its call sounds like "sweet-sweet-sweet."

Pileated woodpecker. Swamp forests are also the home of the brightly hued pileated woodpecker, or logcock. As big as a crow, the pileated sports a red crest on its head, a black back, and black and white feathers underneath. It makes a loud drumming sound as it pecks trees for insects. The pileated's "cuk-cuk-cuk-cuk" call sounds like a high-pitched lawnmower engine.

Snakes and Alligators

Few creatures evoke as much fear as snakes.

Some people shy away from canoe trips on thickly vegetated rivers because of the chance that a snake may drop from an overhanging branch onto their lap. Others shoot every snake on sight, because they think they are killing the poisonous water moccasin or because they regard all snakes, harmful or not, as targets of opportunity.

There's little need to fear snakes on a canoe trip. First, most snakes canoeists will see are nonpoisonous. Second, snakes will try to escape if given the chance.

Of the 49 varieties of snake found in the state, six are poisonous, according to the South Carolina State Museum. The most common, the copperhead, is found throughout the state. It is pinkish to coppery tan, with dark brown hourglass-shaped crossbands around its body. This is the poisonous snake campers are most likely to see. The other five are the Eastern diamondback rattlesnake, the timber (or canebrake) rattlesnake, the pigmy rattlesnake, the coral snake, and the Eastern cottonmouth or water moccasin.

The moccasin is frequently with the brown water snake and, viewed from a distance, few people can tell one from the other. Here are some pointers to help identify the moccasin. Moccasins live in swamps, marshes, and wetlands below the Fall Line but not in the Piedmont or mountains. Dark crossbands with yellowish centers run around their bodies. Their cat-like eyes are set on top of their heads.

All nonpoisonous water snakes have round pupils in eyes set on the sides of their heads. Perhaps the most abundant water snake, and the one canoeists are likely to see most often, is the brown water snake. It has dark brown splotches around its light brown or tan body. The brown water snake likes to bask on low-hanging branches and will usually drop into the water with a "plop" when it senses an approaching boater.

Alligators, as big and vicious-looking as they are, pose little threat to people if left alone. They are found in Lowcountry rivers and marshes, ususally content to stay out of the way of boaters.

Once on the endangered list, these reptiles are on the rebound in South Carolina because of protection from hunting. Alligators are now present in substantial numbers—an estimated 100,000 statewide—in all Lowcountry rivers. The best rivers for gators, in order of alligator population density, are the Edisto, North Santee, Ashepoo, and Combahee.

If you run across an alligator, don't become alarmed. Chances are, the gator will slide into the water or, if already swimming, submerge as your canoe approaches.

American alligator

Green heron

photo courtesy South Carolina Wildlife Magazine

photo by Jack Horan

Brown water snake

Water moccasin

photos courtesy South Carolina Wildlife Magazine

River otter

photos courtesy South Carolina Wildlife Magazine

Fish

A variety of sport fish, from the native brook trout to the striped bass, course South Carolina's rivers from the mountains to the Lowcountry. Gamefish such as the largemouth bass, bluegills, and catfish live in nearly all the warmer freshwater rivers across the state.

Here's a rundown on the more common gamefish and the kind of river they're likely to be found in.

Mountains. The cold-water rivers are home to the brown, rainbow, and brook trout. Brown trout have black spots set against an olive-brown back and generally grow to be the largest of the three trout. Rainbows are marked with black spots over a pinkish-blue and red band across their sides. The diminutive brook trout have greenish, worm-like markings and seldom grow larger than six inches.

Piedmont. Everybody's favorite, the largemouth bass, can be found in Piedmont rivers as well as the sluggish rivers of the Lowcountry. Largemouths have a protruding lower jaw, dark greenish sides and white bellies. Bluegills, a panfish, have dark vertical bands, a slate-blue cheek, and a nearly round shape. Yellow perch are long, slender fish that rarely exceed a pound. White and black crappie are sunfishes that are dappled with black spots; they grow to about two pounds. The striped bass, or rockfish, is silvery with a series of thin stripes running laterally along its side. Striped bass may run 20 pounds or more. The smaller white bass has stripes that are much less pronounced.

Lowcountry. Along with sunfish already described, the ever-popular redbreast sunfish thrives in the blackwater rivers. The redbreast grows up to a pound and has a black gill flap and a bright reddish-orange belly. Another sunfish, the warmouth, is elongated, has red goggle-like eyes, and weighs about four ounces.

South Carolina fishing licenses are sold at more than 1,100 retail stores throughout the state and at state wildlife department offices. For information on fishing laws, write the South Carolina Department of Natural Resources, Box 167, Columbia, SC 29202, or visit the Web site www.dnr.state.sc.us.gov.

Outdoor Hazards and Nuisances

Potential outdoor hazards range from the irritation of biting insects and sunburn to the threat of death that can come from hypothermia, rapid chilling of the body. The prudent canoeist should be aware of these hazards, how to avoid them, and what to do in the event of a mishap.

Lightning and Thunderstorms

The threat of lightning is most likely to occur in warm weather, particularly in summer. Because water is a conductor of electricity, the best course of action for the canoeist when a thunderstorm approaches is to head for shore and get out of the water. Squat on the ground, staying away from high ground and tall trees.

Any canoe can become a shelter in a storm if nothing else is available. Turned over and propped against a tree or a boulder away from the wind, the canoe can provide a refuge from driving rain, hail, and wind and can help ward off hypothermia.

If severe thunderstorms are forecast, postpone the canoe trip. Thunderstorms can spawn tornadoes and flash floods, which can send mountain and Piedmont rivers rising. Most of the Piedmont rivers have shallow beds fed by numerous tributaries. A day or two of heavy rain can rapidly swell them to flood stages.

Water Temperatures

Knowing the approximate temperature of the water in a river helps to make paddlers aware of the potential hazard in a capsize. Falling into the cold waters of a river can lead to hypothermia, which will be discussed in the next section, because water conducts life-supporting body heat away twenty times faster than does air of the same temperature.

While the 70-degree Fahrenheit temperature of a river feels refreshing on a hot summer day, the same river in winter can have water temperatures that fall into the 30s. Such temperatures are life-threatening for the paddler who is immersed for any length of time.

To give an idea of the range of water temperatures over the year, here are average monthly temperatures for the Chattooga, one of the coldest rivers in the state: January, 38 degrees; February, 40 degrees; March, 45 degrees; April, 53 degrees; May, 62 degrees; June, 70 degrees; July, 74 degrees; August, 72 degrees; September, 66 degrees; October, 54 degrees; November, 48 degrees; December, 42 degrees. The temperatures for other South Carolina rivers will generally be warmer than those of the Chattooga.

Hypothermia

Hypothermia is a condition brought on by the rapid loss of body heat from chilling. It may be the most serious river-related threat to paddlers, and it's not confined to cold-weather months. In extreme cases, when the body temperature falls below 90 degrees Fahrenheit, the victim can die.

South Carolina weather is at its most capricious in spring and fall. What can start out as a sunny day can turn into a day with overcast skies and sudden showers in a short time. A rainy day can mean sitting for hours in wet clothing, a condition that can produce hypothermia. The risk can increase in cold-water mountain rivers, such as the Chattooga. It's a good idea to wear an insulating wetsuit on such rivers in the spring and early summer, when water temperatures are still low.

A capsizing or drenching in the winter is especially dangerous. The body loses heat quickly in cold water and even more rapidly if the air temperature is low. Swimming or treading water will speed up the rate of heat loss. The U.S. Coast Guard recommends that boaters attempt to get as much of their bodies out of the water as possible to minimize heat loss by climbing on to their overturned boat. Keep the head out of water since about fifty percent of the heat is lost through that part of the body. Other areas of high heat loss are the neck, groin, and sides. Folding into the fetal position, head, and body bent toward the knees, can help impede heat loss.

A person who has capsized should consider the distance to shore and his or her swimming capabilities before deciding whether to leave an overturned canoe. Canoeists, however, may find themselves on remote rivers where help may not be forthcoming. In that event, use flotation to help move to the shore since the exertion of swimming will step up the loss of body heat.

There are several ways to treat hypothermia victims. The first is to replace wet clothing with dry clothing. If the person shows unmistakable symptoms of hypothermia—uncontrollable trembling and pallor—get him or her to a shelter and a source of warmth immediately. After removing wet clothing, apply heat to the body. Submersion in a tub of warm water is an excellent way to restore body heat, but warm-water baths aren't likely to be available in the wilderness unless a house is nearby. Otherwise, wrap the person in a sleeping bag or tarp.

Frequently, the handiest heat source is another body. Pressing warm, unclothed bodies around the victim can stop the drop in the victim's temperature and can restore body heat.

Give a hypothermia victim warm liquids to drink, easily digested food, but no alcoholic beverages.

Sunburn and Sunstroke

Sunburn is compounded in a canoe because the paddler receives exposure from both the sun's direct rays and from those that reflect off the water.

A few precautions can prevent painful burns. Use a sunscreen with a rating of at least 15; a rating of 30 or higher provides more protection. Wear long-sleeved shirts, hats, and cotton gloves. Avoid wearing shorts or bathing suit—or, if you do, periodically switch to trousers to protect tender thighs and legs. Take long lunch breaks in the middle of the day while the sun is at its peak and its rays are most intense.

Heat exhaustion is advanced dehydration. Give the person water and provide cooling. Heat stroke occurs when the body temperature exceeds 104 degrees F. Immerse the person in cool water and continue to take temperature. Seek medical help.

Biting and Stinging Insects

While insects are the most common outdoor nuisances in South Carolina, some pose a real health threat. Wasps and bees kill more people, through allergic reactions, than poisonous snakes do. Ticks carry dangerous Rocky Mountain Spotted Fever, which is either on the increase in the state or being reported more frequently.

Mosquitoes, gnats, deerflies, and yellowflies are not generally a problem on streams and rivers, especially if a breeze is blowing to keep them scattered. The banks and the surrounding woods are quite another story. Be sure to take some insect repellent if the river trip calls for a jaunt into the woods or an overnight camp. The best repellent is an ointment than contains N,N-diethyl-metatoluamide. It's wise to spray clothing with a spray repellent and apply ointment to exposed skin.

Wasp and hornet stings can be very painful. When stung, scrape the stinger off with a knife or a fingernail and apply an antiseptic. Those persons who are hypersensitive to bee and wasp stings should carry a medically prescribed kit. A tube of hydrocortisone cream is good to have, to relieve the itch of bites and stings.

Remember that bees and wasps are often attracted to colorful garments that bear a flower-like design. Perfumes and colognes also lure biting insects. Bathe with unscented soap before going on a river trip.

Ticks are active in South Carolina during warm-weather months. About one tick in 25 is suspected of being a carrier of Rocky Mountain Spotted Fever, which can kill if not treated properly. Make a thorough examination for ticks at the end of an outing. Remove any tick with pincers or fingers covered with tissue paper. Kill the tick, apply an antiseptic to the bite, and wash the hands with soap and water. Log the date of the tick bite and report any illnesses within two weeks to a physician. The symptoms of Rocky Mountain Spotted Fever are similar to those of the flu—chills, fever, headache, and muscular pains. A spotted rash will break out and spread over the body. If a carrier tick is removed fewer than six hours after it attaches itself to the body, there is usually little chance it will transmit the fever.

Insect repellents can help keep ticks away. To be safe, wear long pants tucked into boots or socks and keep shirts tucked in when walking in tick territory. They like to live in tall grass and weeds. They don't fall out of trees overhanging rivers.

Spiders, Scorpions, and Other Bugs

The black widow and the brown recluse are the only spiders with enough venom to be dangerous to people. Nearly all spiders, however, have a bite that can cause varying degrees of discomfort. The best policy is to watch out for and avoid all spiders.

While scorpions are not rare in South Carolina, encounters with them are. The scorpion's sting is similar to that of a wasp and should be treated similarly.

Caterpillars don't sting but secrete a fluid that can irritate the skin. In early spring of some years, some kinds of caterpillar can be prolific in the trees around blackwater rivers. Wear a long-sleeved shirt just in case. The skin irritations can be treated with hydrocortisone.

Chiggers, or redbugs, frequently hitchhike on those who walk in the woods. Use repellents around the edges of clothing and tuck in shirts and pants to keep these mites from getting on your skin. Mild local anesthetics can relieve itching from chigger bites.

Poison Ivy

The best way to keep from getting a case of poison ivy is to recognize the plant and avoid it. If you're not sure what it looks like, look it up in a wild plant guide, or have someone point it out to you. Poison ivy often grows along river banks and on trees overhanging rivers. It can be identified by the telltale clusters of three bright-green leaves at the end of the stem. Poison ivy has white berries in spring.

After touching poison ivy, rinse the skin immediately with water or soap and water if soap is available. To avoid secondary contamination, remove any clothing that brushed against poison ivy and keep the clothing in a separate bag until it can be washed.

Burns, Broken Bones, and Impure Water

Handle camp stoves, campfires, lanterns, and cooking utensils with care. Treat common burns with cold water or cold compresses, not ice, and cover the affected area with sterile dressing. Don't use butter or ointment on a serious burn.

Don't attempt to set or push a protruding bone back into place. If the victim is bleeding, stop the bleeding with simple, direct pressure, cover the wound and treat the victim for shock. A splint should be bound below and above the break. Seek medical help.

Always carry ample amounts of water. It's almost impossible to tell if surface water is clean enough to drink, even water from pristine mountain streams. Pack purification tablets for emergencies.

Packing a Complete First-Aid Kit

Paddling many river stretches in South Carolina may put boaters miles from the nearest take-out point, which may be considerable time and distance from the nearest medical facility. That's why all paddlers should carry a complete first-aid kit.

A complete first-aid kit should have the following items: soap, space blanket, anti-diarrhea medication, adhesive tape and strips, gauze, antibiotic ointment, antiseptic pads, medically prescribed bee-sting kit for those allergic to insect stings, sunscreen, headache pills, hydrocortisone, sunburn remedy, moleskin (for blisters), calamine lotion, nylon rope, tweezers, knife, lip balm, butane lighter, safety pin, shoelaces, and first-aid manual.

Planning a Canoe Trip

What to Take Canoeing

The first thing to consider before any river trip is the proper canoe for the river. In South Carolina, that means determining whether the river is primarily flatwater with few or no rocks or primarily whitewater with numerous rocks and shoals. Depending on the type of river, paddlers should choose either a canoe designed for flatwater or one designed for whitewater, even though canoes come in dozens of shapes and lengths, solo and tandem.

Flatwater canoes, usually made of a lightweight material like fiberglass, track well (follow a straight line without sliding to the side) and don't curve up radically on the ends. Turned upside down, the rocker (end) curves will be gradual.

Whitewater canoes, on the other hand, are built for maneuverability, flexibility, and structural durability. They are made of high-impact materials such as the compound plastic ABS (acrylonitrile, butadiene, and styrene) or Kevlar that will survive constant pounding against rocks.

Touring kayaks made from molded polyethylene have found their way onto flatwater rivers and lakes.

Each canoe should have a personal flotation device or a lifejacket for each person as well as a throw rope for rescues and a bailer. The throw rope should have a flotation device such as a buoyant cushion or an empty plastic milk container. A plastic one-gallon milk or bleach jug can be fashioned into a bailer by cutting away a portion on the opposite side of the handle to form a scoop.

Whitewater canoes should also be equipped with air bags, which keep the canoe afloat if capsized and aids in displacing water that spills into the boat from standing waves and other turbulence.

Food, Clothing, and Other Gear

A rule of the river is that it's better to have too much food and drink than not enough.

Carrying extra food and water is a precaution against getting stuck on a river longer than you had anticipated. Even if you never take a sip of it, having an extra gallon of water in the canoe can be a comfort, knowing it's there if needed.

Bear in mind that the constant exercise of canoeing burns up a lot of calories.

In addition to sandwich fixings, or whatever lunch may be, it's good to take along an ample supply of quick-energy foods. Granola bars, fruit, gorp (a mixture of dried fruits, nuts, and candy) and raw vegetables like carrots and celery can boost a weary body.

Take a spare set of clothes and a towel and pack them away in a waterproof bag for that unexpected dunking. Pack a second set of shoes for the same reason.

When paddling in cool weather, dress in layers of clothing that can be removed one by one as the day warms up. For cold weather, wear a down jacket, thermal underwear, a light jacket or bulky sweater, thermal socks, heavy gloves, and a knit hat.

The following is a checklist of gear for both day trips and overnight camping trips on the river.

Day trips: Dry bag for maps, hat with brim, long-sleeved shirt, canoe repair kit, first-aid kit, poncho or rain gear, baler or sponge, can opener, rope or twine, whistle, cotton gloves, flashlight, utility knife, waterproof matches, insect repellent, lifejacket, toilet paper, saw or ax, compass, extra batteries, extra paddle, soap and towel, plastic trash bag, extra clothing, sunglasses.

Overnight trips: All of the previous items, plus ground sheet, cookware, extra shoes, stove and fuel, sleeping bag, sleeping pad, tent, lantern, candles, detergent.

Travel Time

First, allow more than you expect the trip will take to avoid getting caught on the river after dark. Plan to complete the trip two hours before dusk to provide additional time for a leisurely float, breaks, miscalculations, and unexpected problems.

Determining float time depends on the length of the section and the conditions of the river. Generally speaking, if a river is deep enough to float a canoe, is fairly free of obstructions, and has a moderate current, most people should be able to do a 15-mile section in six or seven hours.

In South Carolina, it's easier to figure float times on the blackwater rivers. In early spring, however, blackwater rivers carry a lot of water from winter rains and runoffs from feeder swamps, and they move along rapidly. This is an advantage in the lower sections of blackwater rivers where the channels are fairly wide and not so convoluted as are the upper sections. The North Fork and South Fork of the Edisto, for instance, require more time to run at high water because of tricky eddies that constantly push a canoe into brushy banks and tight turns.

The shallow-bedded Piedmont rivers have livelier currents than the blackwater rivers, normally moving at a two-mile-per-hour rate. These rivers also have more gradual bends. Consequently, they can be run faster with less paddling. In late summer, Piedmont rivers tend to shallow out and, with exposed sandbars, travel times become slower.

Calculating float times for whitewater rivers is more complicated. As the difficulty of rapids increases, more time is needed for scouting and regrouping at the end of a rapids run.

In all cases, the earlier you can get onto a river the better your chances of reaching your take-out before darkness falls. In the event you don't succeed in getting off the river before dark, it's wise to carry a flashlight or head lamp to help navigate and spot your landfall.

South Carolina Road Signs

Running shuttles and looking for put-in sites becomes an easier task if you are familiar with the South Carolina road sign system.

South Carolina uses four types of highway signs—the familiar red, white, and blue shields that mark the interstates; the federal highway shields with six points; state highway signs; and secondary highway signs.

State highways use a square sign with the state initials and the highway number, as in S.C. 3.

The highway signs that cause the most confusion are those identifying secondary highways. These small rectangular black signs have white lettering and are always attached to stop signs—never placed at random intervals along the side of the road. Secondary road signs display the letter *S* followed by a hyphen, a one-or two-digit number, another hyphen, and then a number up to four digits.

The letter *S* stands for secondary highway. The first set of numbers indicates the county, and the second set indicates the road number. For example, S-40-863 is the designation for Secondary Highway 863 in Richland County. The same highway might run into another county where the sign would be the same except for the county number. Occasionally, highway numbers change upon entering a different county.

On South Carolina road maps, state highways are designated by outline symbols in the shape of the state with the highway number inside. Secondary highways are marked with encircled highway numbers. To distinguish between the two state highways in this book, they will be referred to in this way: S.C. 3 for state highways; S-863 for secondary highways.

Another road marker paddlers will see is that designating U.S. Forest Service roads. They are marked by a squarish wooden post with the number of the road etched or burned in. Forest Service roads are represented by rectangular outlines on Forest Service maps. They usually do not appear on county road maps.

Before Launching

Float Plan

Making up a float plan helps in a number of ways. It organizes your plans, encourages you to gather helpful information, and gives you a checklist to refer to.

A float plan should include information on water levels, distances of shuttle runs, the name and section of the river, and the put-in and take-out points. List the maps and guides necessary for the trip as well as items such as food and equipment.

Leave a copy of the float plan with a friend or, depending on the difficulty or remoteness of the river, with a forest ranger or wildlife officer.

Legal Rights of Canoeists

The navigable streams and rivers of South Carolina are, by law, public highways. That means canoeists and kayakers may legally float all navigable streams.

State law defines navigable streams as those capable of being navigated by "rafts of lumber or timber." The South Carolina Supreme Court, in a 1908 decision, said that if a waterway has the capacity to be used for commercial purposes, though it is not actually used for such, it is still considered navigable water for pleasure boats.

A 1975 opinion by the South Carolina Attorney General's office, citing previous Supreme Court decisions, said that "a stream navigable in fact is navigable in law. A stream is navigable in fact if a person can float an vessel of any size or construction, for any lawful purpose whatsoever (pleasure or commerce), for any length of the stream, without regard to the ease of difficulty of the stream, so long as the stream is accessible from some public place or terminus."

Just because a stream or river is open to public use doesn't mean the surrounding land is.

On a navigable stream, the river bottom up to the average high watermark belongs to the state. All the land above that watermark should be considered privately owned unless it is known to be part of a county or state park, public boat landing or national forest or park.

River Ethics

River ethics is a matter of common sense and decency.

First, don't litter. Nothing mars a river's natural beauty more than drink cans and other debris strewn about. Make it a practice to carry a plastic garbage bag in each canoe. Remove some of the trash from the river on each trip, leaving the river a prettier place.

Respect signs barring trespassing. Although South Carolina's rivers are open to the public, the land beyond the water's edge is often privately owned. Sometimes the best camping sites are posted. In that event, either push on or try a little tact. Stop and search out the landowner to ask permission to camp overnight. Many, even though their land is posted, appreciate the courtesy and will grant permission.

When camping, whether on private or public lands, don't cut down trees for firewood. Green wood doesn't burn well, and it's the rare site that doesn't have plenty of dead branches and logs within an easy walk. Be sure to bury human waste. Drown fires with water, then cover the ashes with dirt. Leave the campsite cleaner than it was upon arrival.

Boating Regulations

Several South Carolina boating laws apply to canoes and kayaks.

State law requires that boats under sixteen feet must carry U.S. Coast Guard-approved, wearable life jackets for each person aboard. In addition to life jackets, flotation cushions are required for boats sixteen feet and longer.

All "manually propelled vessels" must have a white light on board ready for display in poor lighting to prevent a collision. Lights are required on all boats operating between sunset and sunrise.

Canoe and Kayak Care

Proper care and maintenance can keep canoes and kayaks in good shape for many years.

Most canoes and kayaks are made from fiberglass, Royalex-ABS, polyethylene, or aluminum. While care and maintenance vary from material to material, owners can help preserve the integrity of their boats by following the following recommendations from manufacturers.

Store fiberglass and plastic canoes upside down on a rack or sawhorses in a cool, dry place away from extreme temperatures. Kayaks can be suspended from a wall or rafters. Don't drape a plastic sheet over fiberglass or plastic canoes because a sheet can trap moisture and cause discoloration of the hull. While the ultraviolet rays of the sun cause fiberglass and plastic hulls to deteriorate, aluminum canoes can be stored outside. Don't put them on concrete or earth because those surfaces will speed up oxidation of the metal.

To clean a fiberglass or plastic boat, use a mild detergent or spray cleaner. Wax to spruce up the appearance of the hull. For a more enduring finish, apply a coat of hard wax and buff with a soft cloth. To prevent saltwater corrosion of an aluminum canoe, rinse with fresh water after use in the ocean. Wash with a mild detergent and rub on paste wax to keep the aluminum attractive.

International Scale of River Difficulty

This scale enables the paddler to identify whitewater rapids by their difficulty and danger. The rapids should be considered one class more difficult than listed if the water temperature is below 50 degrees Fahrenheit or if the trip is an extended one in a wilderness area.

Class I: Moving water with a few riffles and small waves; few or no obstructions.

Class II: Easy rapids with waves up to three feet and wide, clear channels that are obvious without scouting. Some maneuvering is required.

Class III: Rapids with high, irregular waves often capable of swamping an open canoe; narrow passages that often require complex maneuvering; waves up to five feet. May require scouting from shore.

Class IV: Long, difficult rapids with constricted passages that often require precise maneuvering and very turbulent waters. Scouting from shore is often necessary, and conditions make rescue difficult. Generally not possible for open canoes; boaters in covered canoes and kayaks should be able to do an Eskimo roll.

Class V: Extremely difficult, long and very violent rapids with highly congested routes that must always be scouted from shore. Rescue conditions are difficult and there is a risk to life in the event of a mishap. The ability to Eskimo roll is essential for covered canoes and kayaks.

Class VI: Difficulties of Class V carried to the extreme of navigability; nearly impossible and very dangerous; only for teams of experts after close study and after all precautions are taken. Definite risk to life.

Canoeist plunges through Seven-Foot Falls on the Chattooga River.

photo by Brian Gomsak

How to Use River Information

Each river trail in this book is accompanied by a narrative description of the trail, a data list, and a map marking off the trail into sections.

The river trails are grouped geographically: Lowcountry, Piedmont and Midlands, and mountains. In all, the trails embrace 30 rivers and their tributaries—for instance, the North Fork, the South Fork, and the main stem of the Edisto River are considered three rivers—for a total distance of more than 1,300 miles.

At the end of the river trails section, the reader will find an abbreviated guide to the larger rivers in the state. These rivers are less desirable for downriver canoeing and kayaking because of numerous dams, extensive lakes, broad expanses of water or the presence of large craft.

River Descriptions

The narrative descriptions of the river trails are based on personal trips and publicly available information on access points and water conditions. They are intended to impart enough logistical data for river running without noting every bend, passage, or rapid.

River Data Lists

The two data lists are snapshots of information to help paddlers plan and carry out a trip.

The access points list, located in an outlined box inside each river map, provides distances and time. The first column gives a letter designation to the major access points on each trail. The access designation appears in the text as well as on the map. The purpose is to break up the river into manageable sections, consisting of several hours of float time. The lettered access points don't always represent put-ins and take-outs in a section. Other access points may be noted in the text as well. The distances between access points are not to scale on the maps. The second column lists mileage between the access points, according to U.S. Geological Survey figures. The third column gives the approximate paddling time for the section. The time is based on experience. Paddlers should factor in additional time for low water, frequent haul-outs, large groups, and scouting for rapids.

The second list, which follows each river narrative, contains technical information about each river. Here is a description of that information.

Topographic maps: These are the detailed topo maps published by the Geological Survey covering the trail sections. The maps contain every bend a river makes but they are often outdated. Many were drawn in the 1940s and don't show newer roads and bridges.

County maps: South Carolina county road maps provide adequate detail for most trips. North Carolina and Georgia county names are also listed for river sections that begin in North Carolina or Georgia.

Average flow: The average flow, based on Geological Survey data, is given both in cubic feet per second and in millions of gallons per hour. The flow indicates the relative size of the river. The volume, however, doesn't tell how fast the river moves. Velocity varies with depth, width, and drop. The Geological Survey doesn't calculate the flow for some rivers in the book. In that case, the entry will read "Not available."

Flood stage: The National Weather Service records flood stages for most of South Carolina's rivers. A list of flood stages and gauge locations is in Appendix A. If no flood stage has been established, the entry will read "Not established."

Gradient: This is the drop in elevation from the first put-in to the last take-out. Gradient gives a guide to river difficulty in terms of water velocity and frequency and magnitude of rapids. Bear in mind a 20-mile-long river with a 100-foot gradient can drop 80 feet in the first 2 miles and only 20 in the remaining 18 miles.

Difficulty: The level of difficulty will be rated by one or several of seven classifications. They are flatwater, fast flatwater, Class I, Class II, Class III, Class IV, Class V. Flatwater means smooth water with a moderate, easy-to-navigate current. Fast flatwater means flatwater with a fast but not turbulent current of three miles per hour or faster. Class I through Class V refers to the International Scale of River Difficulty. These ratings apply to normal or higher-than-normal water levels but not to rivers swollen from heavy rains.

Hazards: These are obstacles that can block, pin, or upset canoes and kayaks. They can be objects such as dams or the partly submerged remnants of bridges. Most often they are logs, exposed snags, overhanging trees, undercut rocks, and life-threatening hydraulics.

Runnable water level: This is a non-technical judgement about the minimum and maximum level of water for a satisfactory run. Low water will turn flatwater trips into a series of lift-and-tug haul-outs over exposed logs and whitewater stretches into seemingly endless rock fields. Rivers become too dangerous at high water; stay off rivers when they approach flood stage.

Suitable for: This is a recommendation for one or more of four skill levels: beginner, intermediate, advanced, and expert. Beginners are paddlers who know the canoe strokes, can maneuver on still or slow flat water, and have some river experience. Intermediates are adept on fast flat water as well as on Class I and Class II waters and, ideally, have several years of paddling under their belts. Advanced paddlers are highly skilled and can competently handle Class III and Class IV whitewater. The highest level, expert, should have sufficient ability, skill, equipment, and experience to negotiate Class V rapids, those so dangerous as to be life-threatening.

photo by Jack Horan

Old-growth bald cypress border Cedar Creek in Congaree National Park.

Part II

1. Chattooga	11. Catawba	21. Four Holes Swamp
2. Chauga	12. Wateree	22. Salkehatchie
3. Tyger	13. Lumber	23. Combahee
4. Enoree	14. Little Pee Dee	24. Okatie-Colleton
5. Broad	15. Lynches	25. Ashepoo
6. Turkey-Stevens Creeks	16. Pocotaligo	26. Ashley
7. Upper Saluda	17. Black	27. Wambaw Creek
8. Lower Saluda	18. South Fork Edisto	28. Santee
9. Congaree	19. North Fork Edisto	29. Waccamaw
10. Congaree Swamp	20. Edisto	30. Cuckhold's Creek

Lowcountry Rivers

Ashepoo
Ashley
Edisto, North Fork
Edisto, South Fork
Edisto, Main Stem
Four Holes Swamp
Little Pee Dee
Lumber

Lynches
Okatie-Colleton
Pocotaligo-Black
Salkehatchie-Combahee
Santee
Waccamaw
Wambaw Creek

photo by Jack Horan

Canoe safari finds campsite on the Salkehatchie River.

Ashepoo River

A Lowcountry tidewater river, the Ashepoo flows through Colleton County into the heart of the ACE Basin, an area rich in wildlife and plantation heritage. The ACE Basin forms where three rivers—Ashepoo, Combahee, and Edisto—enter the Atlantic and spread across 350,000 acres of uplands, freshwater swamps, and saltwater marshes. A combination of private and public ownership and conservation easements had protected 136,000 acres from development by 2005, ensuring the area will remain one of the largest undeveloped estuaries on the East Coast. Depending on the season, paddlers can see bald eagles, wood storks, osprey, ducks, egrets, ibis, tundra swans, raccoons, and alligators.

The Ashepoo (pronounced ASH-eh-poo) begins near Walterboro and flows 40 miles to St. Helena Sound, running a course roughly parallel to the Edisto to the north and to the Combahee to the south. Beforemaking a trip on the Ashepoo, floaters should check the tides because the tidal currents can be strong. Add five to six hours to the Charleston Harbor tides to determine the tide times on the upper Ashepoo. For the section around Mosquito Creek, add 45 minutes.

S.C. 303 to U.S. 17

The first access, albeit not a good one, is at the S.C. 303 bridge (A) 8.3 miles south of Walterboro. A path leads to a suitable throw-in but the only parking available is on the shoulder of the highway. A gravel road just south of the bridge on the east side leads to a number of river houses. It might be possible to arrange to leave a vehicle at one of the house.

The first five miles of the 75.5-mile section are characteristic of a blackwater stream, with twisting turns, overhanging limbs, a narrow channel, and a number of downfalls. Just before the U.S. 17 bridge (B), after Horseshoe Creek joins it from the left, the river widens to about 50 yards. Price's Bridge public landing is 4.0 miles upstream on Horseshoe Creek. The tide influences both creeks.

U.S. 17 to S-26

Below the U.S. 17 bridge, there's a take-out at a commercial landing on the right (west) side. The owners charge a fee.

The next take-out is about 10 miles downriver at Feefarm Creek on the right (west) side that leads to Feefarm Creek Bridge on S-26 (Bennetts Point Road).

After that, paddlers must go another 9 miles to Brickyard public landing on the right (north) side of the S-26 bridge that crosses the Ashepoo.

The Ashepoo turns from fresh water to brackish water over the next 12 miles.

Paddlers should consult a tide table and plan their trip around a midday high tide to make the landing before dark. Catching an outgoing tide about three or four hours after putting in would assure a float time of about eight hours.

While the river widens to about 100 feet just below the U.S. 17 bridge, it's more than 100 yards wide at the S-26 bridge. A narrow fringe of giant cord grass gives way to broad expanses of former rice fields as the river meanders by colonial-era planta-tion homes.

The surviving antebellum houses at Lavington Plantation can be seen on the right side about two hours below U.S. 17. Many of the rice fields and dikes border-ing the Ashepoo date to the early eighteenth century.

S-26 to Bennetts Point Landing

The final take-out, Bennetts Point Landing (D), is 7.0 miles away and 200 yards up Mosquito Creek on the left (east) side. Don't confuse it with Crooked Creek, also on the left but 5.0 miles downstream. Mosquito Creek is much wider and the spars of shrimp boats should be visible across the marsh before reaching Mosquito Creek.

Bennetts Point, a public landing 4.8 miles beyond the S-26 bridge, is on a gravel road a few hundred yards after S-26 ends. Bear to the right at the end of the pave-ment. Although this is the last access on the Ashepoo, it's possible to paddle another four miles to a cut-through on the left (east) side that connects the Ashepoo to the Edisto. Edisto Island is about 3.0 miles away; the Edisto River is about three times wider than the Ashepoo at this point.

Ashepoo River at a Glance
Trail: S.C. 303 to Bennetts Point Landing
Length: 31.6 miles
Topographic Maps: Bennetts Point, Green Pond,
        Walterboro
County Maps: Colleton
Average Flow: Not available
Flood Stage: Not established
Gradient: 10 feet, or 0.3 feet per mile
Difficulty: Flat tide water
Hazards: Some downfalls and strainers in the first
        section, tides and wind in the lower section
Runnable Water Level: Runnable year-round
Suitable For: Beginners

Ashley River

From its modest origins in Dorchester County to its broad embrace with Charleston Harbor, the Ashley River cuts a scenic and historical path through the state's largest port city. The charm of the Ashley is rooted in its historical aura, and a city that prides itself on three centuries of development hardly intrudes on much of this 19.5-mile trail. The section from U.S. 17A to Mark Clark Expressway has been designated as a state Scenic River.

About 1.5 miles of the upper part of the river near Summerville and the lower 3.0 miles are rather heavily developed with homes, private docks, and a golf course. Although Charleston's industrial hub is close by, the Ashley is hardly affected by it, nor is the paddler cognizant of the sprawling city. In fact, the paddler sees nothing of the Charleston skyline until passing a railroad trestle 1.3 miles from the take-out at County Farm Landing at the end of the trail.

The float trip affords capitvating views of old river houses and elegant modern homes. The major architectural attractions are plantation houses at Charleston's famous gardens, Middleton Place and Magnolia Plantation, as well as Drayton Hall, Millbrook, and Runnymede.

Ecologically, the river offers several miles of unspoiled marshlands on one side and fallow rice fields on the other. Wildlife is abundant, especially wading birds and shore birds, despite the nearness of the city. On warm spring and early summer days, it's not improbable for paddlers to spot several large alligators sunning themselves on the edge of the marsh.

There are three ways to approach paddling the Ashley.

The first is doing only the 3.0-mile segment from S.C. 165 near Summerville to Old Dorchester State Park, or paddle an additional half mile to Jessen Landing.

The second is paddling the 14.5 miles from the park to the County Farm Landing near the Mark Clark Expressway. This option entails figuring tide tables and running the risk of being pushed around by winds on the lower section where the river is up to 500 yards wide.

The third approach involves planning a float trip around the tides. Catch an outgoing tide about an hour after high tide, float from Old Dorchester down to Magnolia Plantation, then take a lunch break and ride the incoming tide back to the park.

It's difficult to figure float times because the elements of wind and tide in the lower sections are problematical. Generally, allot six to seven hours for the float from Old Dorchester State Park to County Farm Landing. If you start an hour before high tide, you'll find it's easier to deal with an incoming tide in the upper section where the river is not very wide and wind is not so much a factor.

S.C. 165 to Colonial Dorchester State Historic Site

Put in at S.C. 165 (A) 0.5 mile past the intersection with S.C. 642, about 1.0 mile south of Summerville. The access is a throw-in on the right (west) side of the river above the bridge. There is an unpaved parking area just off the highway.

This 3.0-mile section is narrow and twisting with some overhangs. It has many of the characteristics of a blackwater river, but the water is brackish and tides can run as much as four feet. Take out at Colonial Dorchester State Historic Site (B) on the left (east) bank. The ruins of the old fort should be visible from the river, but there is no landing or beach.

Construction of the fort was authorized in 1757 as an outer ring of defense for Charles Town during the French and Indian War. The walls were made of tabby, a mixture of oyster shells, lime, and sand.

Another half mile is Jessen Landing on the left (east) bank, off S.C. 642.

Colonial Dorchester State Historic Site to County Farm Landing

The state park is situated at the end of S-373 off S.C. 642, east of Summerville. Canoes must be portaged about 100 feet from the parking area to the river.

This section covers 14.5 miles to the end of the trail at County Farm Landing (C). Although there are lands between these access points, they are private. There is some high ground on the left bank where paddlers may get out and stretch their legs, but no camping areas. The wildlife refuge and the plantations all are posted against trespassing.

About 1.5 miles downstream from the state park, King's Grant Golf Course on the left and Mateeba Gardens on the right are visible. Then comes a long stretch where there is little development. Middleton Place appears about 3.0 miles down on the right, and Magnolia Plantation is another 5.5 miles. Millbrook and Runnymede are also on that stretch.

The final 3.0 miles is wide with fewer bends, and the river is flanked by broad marshes. Take out at County Farm Landing on the left (east) about 100 yards below the Mark Clark Expressway bridge.

To reach the landing, take Leeds Avenue from Mark Clark Expressway or Dorchester Road (S.C. 642). There is ample parking at the public landing.

Ashley River at a Glance

Trail: S.C. 165 to County Farm Landing

Length: 17.5 miles

Topographic Maps: Charleston, Johns Island,
     Ladson, Stallsville

County Maps: Charleston, Dorchester

Average Flow: Not available

Flood Stage: Not established

Gradient: 10 feet, or 0.5 feet per mile

Hazards: Tides and winds below Colonial
Dorchester State Historic Site

Runnable Water Level: Runnable year-round

Suitable For: Beginners accompanied by
intermediates below Colonial Dorchester
State Historic Site

Edisto River

The Edisto is one of the most enchanting and popular blackwater rivers in South Carolina. The river has four parks along its banks and numerous access points, yet its luxuriant foliage, sandy beaches, and tea-colored water remains relatively undisturbed. From its upper reaches just above the Fall Line in the west-central part of the state to its mouth at St. Helena Sound south of Charleston, the Edisto travels more than 200 miles through portions of eight counties and drains 3,110 square miles comprising 10 percent of the state.

Two main tributaries, the North Fork and the South Fork, make up the Edisto. Their confluence below Orangeburg forms the main stem of the river. The North Fork winds through Aiken, Lexington, and Orangeburg Counties. The longer South Fork begins in Aiken County and passes through Barnwell and Bamberg Counties. The main stem courses 100 miles through Colleton, Dorchester, and Charleston Counties before splitting into the North Edisto and South Edisto Rivers in the coastal marshes.

Besides the two forks, the other major tributary is Four Holes Swamp, which enters near Givhans Ferry State Park in Dorchester County.

The Edisto (pronounced ed-iss-TOE) was named after a tribe of Indians that inhabited the mainland and islands along the river's lower course. The river was a significant transportation and shipping route for planters and traders in the eighteenth and nineteenth centuries, linking the interior with the coast and the port city of Charleston.

To shorten the distance, architect Robert Mills and others devised a plan to build a 14-mile-long canal that would connect the Edisto with the Ashley River, which flows through Charleston. In his 1825 *Mills' Atlas of South Carolina* Mills wrote that the canal "would save 80 miles of difficult, and in some places dangerous navigation, between the Upper Edisto and Charleston." The canal was never built.

In 1865, the North Fork was the scene of a skirmish between Confederate and Union troops. Six hundred Confederates defended the Edisto River bridge, the present site of Edisto Memorial Gardens in Orangeburg. They temporarily halted the advance of the right wing of the Union Army commanded by Gen. W. T. Sherman.

Wildlife is abundant, with protonotary warblers, downy woodpeckers, and red-shouldered hawks along the upper sections, and wood storks, osprey, and alligators along the lower sections. The Edisto is well-known among anglers for its redbreast sunfish.

Fifty-six miles of the river has been designated as the Edisto Canoe and Kayak Trail, beginning at Whetstone Crossroads (U.S. 21 at S.C. 61). The trail includes two state parks and several landings that provide for a variety of paddling opportunities from a half-day trip to overnighters. For information on guided trips and the annual Edisto Riverfest, call (843) 549-9595.

The North Fork, the South Fork, and the main stem of the Edisto trails cover 206.4 miles.

North Fork

This 52.2-mile trail begins at Carson Park at the U.S. 321 bridge (A). Put in south of the bridge at a turnoff by a park sign. The North Fork Blueway, a 33.0-mile canoe trail, begins 9.0 miles upstream at S.C. 3 and ends at Glover Street Landing near U.S. 301-601 in Orangeburg.

U.S. 321 to S-73

The 5.2-mile section is marked by sharp turns, low-hanging trees, deadfalls, and brush extending into the channel. About two hours downstream is the S-73 bridge (B), which has a concrete ramp and a parking area at Slab Landing on the right (south) side of the river below the bridge.

S-73 to S-74

From here, the North Fork picks up more of the twists and turns that are characteristic of the reaches below Orangeburg.

The river has several spots that are closed in with bushes or blocked with logs, requiring heads-down maneuvering.

The 8.0-mile section ends at S-74 (C), Shillings Bridge. Take out at Baughman's Landing on the left (north) side, just above the bridge.

photo by Jack Horan

Kayakers assemble for float on the North Fork of the Edisto River.

S-74 to U.S. 301-601

One of the most popular stretches on the Edisto is the seven-mile run between Shillings Bridge and Edisto Memorial Gardens in Orangeburg.

Edisto Gardens offers an alternate take-out for those who don't want to float the additional quarter of a mile to the U.S. 301-601 bridge (D). Look for a beach on the left bank at the upper part of the park. Below the bridge is Glover Street Public Landing on the left (east) side of the river.

U.S. 301-601 to S-39

This 12.3-mile section is one of the most remote and primitive parts of the Edisto. Beyond the first three or four miles, the river is so strewn with logs and deadfalls that it is passable by canoe only.

Between Orangeburg and S-39 (E), the river is bounded by swamp forest and has a narrow, twisting channel. Novices shouldn't attempt this trip unless accompanied by experienced paddlers because of the many deadfalls and unpredictable currents.

Normally, the current is moderately swift on both forks in late winter and spring. There are numerous in-flows, however, that create tricky eddies. When the water is high after heavy rains, be prepared for quick maneuvering.

At the S-39 bridge, take out at Rowes public landing on the right (west) side above the bridge.

S-39 to U.S. 21

It's 22.7 miles to the U.S. 21 bridge. There's no take-out at the S-63 bridge, the last highway that crosses the North Fork.

Below the confluence with the South Fork, paddlers can take out at the U.S. 78 bridge or at a landing at the end of S-434.

The S-63 bridge is 1.7 miles above the confluence. After the confluence, the river widens and several houses appear on the right bank.

At U.S. 21 (F), the access to a private landing is on the right (west) side above the bridge. The owner charges a small fee.

⌐╼╾┐ North Fork Edisto River at a Glance

Trail: U.S. 321 to U.S. 21 on Edisto River

Length: 55.2 miles

Topographic maps: Orangeburg, St. Matthews,
    Woodford

County Maps: Bamberg, Orangeburg

Average Flow: 794 cubic feet per second or 21.4

million gallons per hour at U.S. 301-601

Flood Stage: 8 feet at U.S. 301-601 (Orangeburg)

Gradient: 100 feet or 2.0 feet per mile

Difficulty: Fast flatwater in late winter and early
spring on upper sections; flatwater otherwise

Hazards: Strainers, tight turns, downfalls,
overhangs. tricky eddies at high water

Runnable Water Level: Sections above Shilllings
Bridge may be almost impassable during late
summer

Suitable For: Intermediates on upper sections;
beginners from Shillings Bridge and below

South Fork

The South Fork trail covers 64.5 miles, concluding at U.S. 21.

S-53 to S.C. 3

Start at the S.C. 53 bridge (A) at Aiken State Park, except during low-water periods. Experienced paddlers who don't mind tight squeezes, occasional haul-outs, and other navigation problems will enjoy this 15.2-mile section. Conditions on the river change constantly, so carry a brush ax, extra food and water, and a light in case of delays.

Below S-53, the first landmark is Davis Bridge, which connects a gravel road (S-212) 6.3 miles away. Keadle's Bridge on S-22 is 2.3 miles farther. A public landing at the S-39 bridge is 5.3 miles away, followed by the S.C. 3 bridge (B) another 6.6 miles. This is a throw-in on the left (north) side.

S.C. 3 to U.S. 321

A half-mile below the S.C. 3 bridge is Hog Pen Landing.

The 12.7-mile float to U.S. 321 (C) can be made in six hours. It still may be necessary to call on the bush ax a few times and perhaps do some deft maneuvering over fallen logs.

The landing at U.S. 321 bridge is closed to private use. Use Claude's Landing at the end of S-365 about 1.4 miles below the bridge on the right (south) side.

U.S. 321 to U.S. 301-601

The next few miles offer plenty of access points, and the channel begins to widen and deepen.

After Claude's Landing, the next landing is 2.3 miles away at the S.C. 70 bridge on the left (north) side above the bridge. The road to Ness Landing is about one-fourth mile north of the bridge.

Bobcat Landing at U.S. 301-601 (D) is 5.7 miles farther. A parking lot and paved access are on the right (south) side just before the bridge.

U.S. 301-601 to S-39-42

This 4.7-mile section marks the last take-out on the South Fork before its confluence with the North Fork.

Take out at the S-39-42 bridge (E), Cannon's Bridge, on the right (south) side below the bridge. This is Brabham's Landing.

S-39-42 to S-434

From S-39-42, it's 9.6 miles to the confluence. The main steam widens to 30 or 40 yards before narrowing again and braiding into tight passages about a mile and a half above U.S. 21. Here, it is prudent to follow markers with red arrows to keep from dead-ending in oxbow lakes. If you have sufficient time, however, exploring these sloughs can be intriguing.

The U.S. 78 bridge is 4.8 miles downstream but lacks an adequate take-out. Just 1.4 miles beyond is Zig Zag Landing at the end of S-434 (F) on the right (south) side.

S-434 to U.S. 21

The last section, 6.7 miles long, parallels S.C. 61 to the south, within range of highway noise. Take out at the private landing on the right (south) side just before the U.S. 21 bridge (G). The owner charges a small fee.

South Fork Edisto River at a Glance
Trail: S-53 at Aiken State Park to U.S. 21 on
    Edisto River
Length: 64.5 miles
Topographic Maps: Bamberg, Orangeburg,
    Seivern, Williston, Woodford
County Maps: Aiken, Bamberg, Barnwell,
    Orangeburg
Average Flow: 787 cubic feet per second or 21.2
    million gallons per hour at U.S. 321
Flood Stage: Not established

Gradient: 170 feet or 2.6 feet per mile
Difficulty: Fast flatwater on upper sections at high
    water; flatwater otherwise
Hazards: Strainers, tight turns, downfalls,
    overhangs, tricky eddies at high water
Runnable Water level: Runnable year-round
Suitable For: Intermediates above U.S. 301-601,
    beginners below that point

Main Stem
U.S. 21 to U.S. 15

This is the beginning of an 87.6-mile trail that ends in the coastal marshlands.

Put in at the U.S. 21 bridge (A), Sandy Island Bridge, at Whetstone Crossroads in Colleton County. The 21.9-mile run to Colleton State Park at U.S. 15 is mostly open river with numerous sandbars (when water levels are normal or low) and a mix of swamp and upland forest. Oxbows provide interesting side trips and sandy, pine-studded bluffs, some 30 feet high, offer contrast to the swamps.

Much of this largely undeveloped stretch is among the prettiest on the Edisto or any other blackwater river in the state. Birdlife, such as wood ducks, pileated woodpeckers, and kingfishers, is plentiful.

The only bridge along the way is I-95, about two hours above U.S. 15 (B). Simmons Landing, a private fee landing off S.C. 61, is about 2.0 miles north of I-95.

Below I-95 is the Canady's power plant, whose cooling towers are so close to the river paddlers may be sprayed with harmless mist.

At U.S. 15, pull out at Colleton State Park on the right (west) bank or at the T. Coke Weeks public boat landing on the left (east) bank.

U.S. 15 to S-21-29

The Edisto runs 20.3 miles from Colleton State Park to Givhans Ferry State Park.

The first part of this run is a 7.7-mile segment to S-21-29 bridge, Stokes Bridge, (C). About four miles below the state park is a treacherous section where the river narrows. Watch out for overhangs and submerged trees in the swift current.

The landing has been closed to the public, so paddlers must proceed to S.C. 61.

S-21-29 to S.C. 61

Four miles below the S-29 bridge is Cane Island, the first landmark on this 12.6-

mile section. The narrow channel on the right can furnish a quick run through lively riffles when the water is high.

Mars Oldfield Landing is about 6.0 miles farther on the right. With the exception of three sweeping bends, the river straightens and widens. Four Holes Swamp River enters from the left 2.4 miles before Givhans Ferry State Park.

Moderate bluffs on the left mark the approach of the park. Take out where a beach comes into view just above the S.C. 61 bridge (D).

S.C. 61 to West Bank Landing

From Givhans Ferry State Park, it's 28.8 miles to West Bank Landing (F). Paddlers, however, can get on and off the Edisto at several points.

The first is T. W. Messervy Landing on the left (north) side, about 3.0 miles downstream.

It's 4.4 more miles to Good Hope Landing on the right (west) bank off S-91 and 2.0 miles farther to Long Creek Landing on the same side. Both Good Hope and Long Creek public landings in Colleton County can be reached from S-91.

There is a private landing on the left (east) side at U.S. 17A. A half mile below U.S. 17A is Sullivan's Ferry Landing, also on the left (east) side. Lowndes Landing is about 4.0 miles downstream on the same side.

Martin's Landing, another public landing, is 7.2 miles away on the left (east) side of S-38 in Charleston County. The terrain varies from pine bluffs to swamp forest along this section. Drayton Swamp drains into the river from Dorchester County below U.S. 17A, and Tupelo Swamp flows in from Colleton County.

U.S. 17 is 8.0 miles below Martin's Landing. The highway has no access to the river however, putting the next take-out at West Bank Landing, 1.9 miles farther. West Bank, as its name indicates, is a public landing on the west (right) side off S-30, 3.7 miles south of U.S. 17.

Below U.S. 17 at Jacksonboro, Snuggedy Swamp comprises a wild and undeveloped tract between the Edisto and Ashepoo Rivers.

West Bank Landing to Dawhoo Bridge Landing

The last recommended section of the Edisto is an 18.5-mile run from West Bank Landing to Dawhoo Landing (G) on the Intracoastal Waterway.

About 5.0 miles downriver, on the left and a mile up Penny Creek, is Penny Creek public landing, off S-38. Willtown Bluff Landing is another 5.0 miles downstream on the left side, also off S-38. Dawhoo Bridge Landing is off S.C. 174, about 3.0 miles south of S.C. 174 in Charleston County.

The paddler should not confuse the Dawhoo River with the Intracoastal Waterway, although both channels lead to the landing. The Dawhoo River is more narrow and twisting than the Edisto, which widens into a broad, meandering river about 7.0 miles below U.S. 17. The Dawhoo connects with the Edisto 10.1 miles below West Bank Landing.

The Intracoastal Waterway is another 5.0 miles downstream where a horseshoe bend bears west, south, then east. A mile up the Waterway is a shell ramp at the end of a gravel road that leads to S-174. It's another 1.5 miles up the Waterway to Dawhoo Bridge Landing.

This section is strongly affected by tides, so it's imperative to catch an outgoing tide to avoid a strenuous workout. Sea birds and wading birds are abundant on the lower Edisto and the saltwater environment is markedly different from that upstream.

A number of plantations flank the river, most notably Hutton Plantation at the site of Willtown, a town that was settled in 1697 and flourished through the age of rice plantations. No trace of it remains today, although evidence of the rice fields can be seen.

Edisto River at a Glance

Trail: U.S. 21 to Dawhoo Bridge Landing on S-174

Length: 86.7 miles

Topographic maps: Bennetts Point, Cottageville, Edisto Island, Fenwick, Lodge, Ridgeville, St. George

County Maps: Charleston, Colleton, Dorchester

Average Flow: 2,662 cubic feet per second or 71.7 million gallons per hour at S.C. 61

Flood Stage: 10 feet at S.C. 61 (Givhans Ferry)

Gradient: 90 feet or 1.0 feet per mile

Difficulty: Flatwater on upper sections, tidewater on lower section

Hazards: Occasional snags and strainers above Colleton State Park, wind and tide on lower section

Runnable Water Level: Runnable year round

Suitable For: Beginners on all but lower section, which requires intermediate experience

Four Holes Swamp

Four Holes Swamp can be paddled in two different parts, each a distinctive blackwater experience. You can float the stream to the Edisto River or you can take a guided tour of the National Audubon Society's sanctuary in the Francis Beidler Forest.

The swamp's name is thought to have come from four bubbling, bottomless holes in its interior. Other accounts cited four holes that were formed by seasonally dry passages early settlers used to cross the swamp.

The Four Holes Swamp stream connects a number of small lakes or "holes" in Calhoun County, then meanders through Orangeburg and Dorchester Counties for 62 miles before emptying into the Edisto River.

The stream passes through a swamp of cypress and tupelo mixed with occasional bluffs forested with oak, magnolia, and bay trees. While the stream is easy to follow, downed trees obstruct the channel in places. Pick a time when the water level is neither too high nor too low because debris in the narrow channels can create a danger in high water and cause untold haul-outs in low water.

U.S. 78 to S-56

The first possible put-in is at the U.S. 78 bridge (A) between Dorchester and Summerville. U.S. 78 intersects with U.S. 178 about 100 yards west of the river. You may put in at a private landing on the north side of the bridge for a small fee.

Hidden in the brush near the bridge is a historical marker that describes the area as the site of an eighteenth-century causeway built in 1753 following the passage of an appropriations act. This was also the site of a patriot post during the Revolutionary War where several skirmishes were fought. It was here on July 14, 1781, that Col. Henry Hampton and a small American force cut off the British retreat from Orangeburg.

The stream is fairly open for the first mile of this 5.2-mile section, then it narrows. The first landmark is a railroad at 1.9 miles. About three miles farther, the stream widens into Steed's Lake. The S-56 bridge, Horse Ford Bridge, (B) is 15 minutes away.

Take out at the landing below the S-56 bridge on the left (south) side.

S-56 to Givhans Ferry State Park

After the S-56 bridge, the stream begins to get tricky, braiding into small rivulets, some of which lead to dead ends. Carry a hatchet or saw.

It's 3.5 miles to the S-19 bridge and 0.4 miles after that to the confluence with the Edisto. The float down the Edisto to Givhans Ferry State Park is 2.4 miles. Take out on the left (east) bank at a swimming beach. If you come to the S-61 bridge, you've floated too far.

Francis Beidler Forest

The Francis Beidler Forest is located east of I-26 on nearly 12,000 acres owned and managed by the National Audubon Society in Four Holes Swamp. Within the sanctuary are 1,800 acres of virgin bald cypress-tupelo forest, one of the largest remaining tracts in the world.

The Audubon property is above U.S. 78. Paddlers are not allowed to begin floats in the Francis Beidler Forest and continue down Four Holes Swamp.

The sanctuary is open to the public from 9 a.m. to 5 p.m. daily except Mondays, Thanksgiving Day, and December 24, 25, and 31. An admission is charged. Visitors can walk out into the swamp on a 1.5-mile-long boardwalk.

Naturalist-led guided canoe tours are available when water levels are high enough. Although paddling isn't difficult, participants should know how to handle a canoe. The main hazard is poison ivy.

Visitors may see alligators, water snakes, turtles, and birds such as yellow-crowned night herons, barred owls, and wood ducks.

For information on water levels in the swamp, call the sanctuary at (843) 462-2150. For other information, write the sanctuary at Francis Beidler Forest, 336 Sanctuary Road, Harleyville, SC 29448.

To get to the sanctuary, exit I-26 at S.C. 453 or S.C. 27 and follow the signs posted on U.S. 78-178.

Four Holes Swamp at a Glance

Trail: U.S. 78 to Givhans Ferry State Park

Length: 11.5 miles

Topographic Maps: Maple Cane Swamp, Pringletown, Ridgeville

County Maps: Colleton, Dorchester

Average Flow: Not available

Flood Stage: Not established

Gradient: 5 feet, or 0.4 feet per mile

Difficulty: Flatwater

Hazards: Deadfalls, strainers, blocked channels

Runnable Water Level: May be impassable in late summer and fall; high water levels can make stream dangerous.

Suitable For: Beginners accompanied by
intermediates.

Little Pee Dee River

The Little Pee Dee is one of South Carolina's most striking blackwater rivers, a gently meandering stream that forms a haven for fish and wildlife in the upper coastal plain.

The lower 14 miles of the Little Pee Dee, from U.S. 378 to the confluence with the Great Pee Dee, has been designated as a State Scenic River. In 2005, another 48 miles, all in Dillon County, were designated.

Along the upper part of the river, a string of state-owned lands protect part of a corridor from just above the confluence with the Lumber River near Nichols to the area between U.S. 501 and U.S. 378. The Little Pee Dee River Heritage Preserves are open to the public year-round and camping is allowed.

The river's scenic values are high. "The Little Pee Dee is at one moment a broad stream, then divides and subdivides into several channels that flow through the swamp or around islands," wrote the South Carolina Water Resources Commission in supporting the eligibility of the river for scenic river status. ". . . Once out of the range of powerboats, the quiet and stillness of the river present a hushed atmosphere of wilderness, broken only by the quiet murmur of gently flowing water, the splash of a frog, or the call of waterfowl."

The river was named after an Indian tribe called the Pee Dees, about whom little is known. The Pee Dees seem to have disappeared around the 1740s, possibly by assimilation into the Catawba nation to the west.

During the Revolutionary War, the Little Pee Dee was a center of activity for Gen. Francis Marion, the Swamp Fox, who fought the British with guerrilla warfare tactics. In one battle near Galivants Ferry on September 4, 1780, Marion scored a major victory over 200 Tories.

Like other South Carolina rivers, the Little Pee Dee was an important highway of commerce in the 1800s. As late as 1915, steamboats ran upriver to Galivants Ferry, where U.S. 501 now crosses.

One of the river's most abundant mammals is the beaver. The large rodents have reestablished themselves on the upper parts of the river. Birds such as wood ducks, pileated woodpeckers, and prothonotary warblers are common.

The Little Pee Dee is like two rivers, changing character at the confluence with the Lumber. The upper part is a small, twisting channel cluttered with trees, limbs, and snags. The lower part is wide and open except for several tight spots near U.S. 378.

The 103.6-mile trail begins at S-23 in Dillon County and concludes at two access points on the Great Pee Dee in Horry and Marion Counties.

S-23 to U.S. 301-501

The Little Pee Dee looks deceptively wide at the S-23 bridge, Harley's Bridge, (A) 0.8 miles north of S.C. 90, northwest of Dillon. But the river narrows in a quarter of a mile or so, assuming the coiling passages typical of the upper sections. At some points, the river is 20 feet wide or less, making boating difficult.

After about a mile, the river appears to fork. Bear to the right.

An alternate put-in is Moccasin's Bluff public landing at the end of S-437, about 3.0 miles downstream.

Below I-95, the nearly continuous litter of trees and limbs festooned with poison ivy make the going slow.

At the U.S. 301-501 bridge (B), take out on the left (north) side just beyond the bridge.

U.S. 301-501 to S-45

The first landmark along this stretch is the S.C. 9 bridge 4.0 miles away. Below the bridge, the river widens and straightens, forming sloughs among the cypresses. Some mature trees, with a girth of 12 feet or so, stand along the banks and in the channel.

Beavers are common along this section and paddlers who slip through quietly at dusk may catch a glimpse of the animals swimming.

The Pee Dee Park landing is 3.9 miles below the S.C. 9 bridge on the right (west) shore. From Dillon go south on S.C. 57 for 3.2 miles and turn left at a dirt road just before a small store.

The other take-out is 4.2 miles downstream at the S-45 bridge (C), which is less than a mile north of S.C. 57 at Floydale. Take out on the left (north) side above the bridge.

S-45 to U.S. 76

Below S-45, the next bridge is 4.0 miles away at S-22 on the edge of the Little Pee Dee State Park. There is no access, though a canoeist could haul out through the woods if necessary.

From that point, the Little Pee Dee enters an isolated swamp forest marked by sloughs, false channels, and debris. The work of beavers, in the form of chiseled trees and stripped saplings, is everywhere.

S.C. 41, about five miles below the park, offers an intermediate take-out. Look for the landing on the right (west) side below the bridge.

The next bridge is at S-72, a dirt road 5.6 miles east of S.C. 41 near Fork. The S-72 bridge is 6.0 miles downstream from S.C. 41. Take out on the right (west) side below the bridge.

At the S-60 bridge 4.0 miles away, the access is on the right (west) side above the bridge.

The U.S. 76 bridge (D) is 2.7 miles farther. Access is on the right (west) side below the bridge, but the owner charges a small fee.

U.S. 76 to S.C. 917

A mile below the bridge, the Lumber River enters from the left. At that point, the river widens considerably and loses its swampy characteristics. River houses become more frequent.

Two public landings are on the west side of the river. The first is Gilcrest, about a mile below U.S. 76 on S-319. Next is Red Bluff No. 1 at the end of S-593 off S-31.

The S-917 bridge, Sandy Bluff Bridge, (E) is 6.3 miles south of the confluence. Take out on either side.

S.C. 917 to U.S. 501

The river broadens into a succession of wide spots, known as lakes, bordered by a forest of cypress, pine, and hardwoods.

Cartwheel Public Landing, 5.4 miles downriver, is on the right (west) side at the end of a dirt road that intersects S.C. 41 and S-91 south of Mullins. Cartwheel is 4.7 miles from U.S. 501.

At the U.S. 501 bridge (F) at Galivants Ferry, the Little Pee Dee constricts into a smaller channel. A ramp is on the right (west) side below the bridge.

U.S. 501 to U.S. 378

This is the longest stretch of the river between bridges: 29.3 miles. Paddlers can choose from among eight landings to get on or off the river, from either the Horry or Marion County side.

The first, Huggins, is about 2.0 miles below U.S. 501 on the Horry County side. Also called Cook Landing, it is off S-216.

About 3.0 miles farther on the Marion County side is Knife Island Landing. Davis Landing is another mile. Each is off the same dirt road off S.C. 41, about 2.7

miles south of U.S. 501 junction.

Locust Tree Landing, 13.7 miles below U.S. 501, is on the Marion County side and can be reached from a dirt road off S.C. 908, about 1.5 miles south of the S.C. 41 junction.

On the Horry County side, Gunter's Lake Landing is about a mile below Locust Tree Landing. This landing is 8.0 miles south of U.S. 501, off S-99.

White Oak then Watson's Landing are about 3.0 miles downriver on the Marion County side, off S-86 or Bay Road.

Hughes Landing on the Horry County side is about 3.0 miles farther, off S-99.

At U.S. 378 (G), take out on the left (east) side at Pitt Landing.

Drifting by river houses on the Little Pee Dee River

U.S. 378 to Tan Yard Landing

The river resumes its swampy appearance around U.S. 378, winding for the first 5.0 miles or so beyond the bridge. The State Scenic River designation begins here.

About 4.0 miles downstream on the Marion County side is Sampson Landing, off the river on Sampson Lake and accessible from S-49, Woodbury Road.

Punch Bowl Landing, another 4.0 miles, is on the right (east) side, at the end of a dirt road that begins at the intersection of S-24 and S-135 south of Conway.

The last two landings, Sanders and Parkers, are off S-49, on the right (west) side of Russ Creek off the Little Pee Dee. Along this stretch the river begins to broaden in the delta preceding the confluence with the Great Pee Dee, which enters from the right.

To reach Tan Yard Landing (H), go upstream on the Great Pee Dee for a mile. The landing is on the right (north) bank at the end of S-49.

U.S. 378 to U.S. 701

For paddlers who want to go on to the next bridge, U.S. 701 (I) is 4.9 miles downstream from the confluence with the Great Pee Dee. It is also called the Yauhannah Bridge. Take out on the left (north) side above the bridge.

Little Pee Dee River at a Glance

Trail: S-23 to U.S. 701 on Great Pee Dee River

Length: 103.6 miles

Topographic Maps: Centenary, Dillon East, Dillon West, Dongola, Fork, Galivants Ferry, Johnsonville, Lake View, Nichols, Yauhannah

County Maps: Dillon, Georgetown, Horry, Marion

Average Flow: 3,148 cubic feet per second or 84.8 million gallons per hour at U.S. 501

Flood Stage: 9 feet at U.S. 501 (Galivants Ferry)

Gradient: 90 feet, or 0.9 feet per mile

Difficulty: Flat water

Hazards: Deadfalls, strainers, and snags above U.S. 76

Runnable Water Level: Runnable year-round; sections above U.S. 76 may be impassable in low water.

Suitable For: Beginners accompanied by intermediates above U.S. 76; otherwise, beginners.

Lumber River

The Lumber River rises in Moore County, North Carolina, and meanders through South Carolina's Sandhills region and surrounding swamps before joining the Little Pee Dee River near Nichols.

In North Carolina, the small, twisting Lumber is a favorite of blackwater paddlers. The state designated part of the Lumber as North Carolina's first canoe trail. In 1998, the federal government elevated the Lumber to national prominence, declaring 81 miles as a National Wild and Scenic River. The lower segment extends to the South Carolina state line. The N.C. Division of Parks and Recreation has begun purchasing land along the river and eventually hopes to protect the entire corridor through state and local park lands, conservation easements, and donations.

The beginning point of this trail is N.C. 904 near the town of Fair Bluff. Below N.C. 904, the Lumber presents a panorama of mixed forest—bald cypress, pines, and hardwoods flank the river. Beaver live along the banks. Paddlers may flush out great blue herons, wood ducks, and wild turkeys.

N.C. 904 to U.S. 76

The first put-in at the N.C. 904 bridge (A) is the last highway entrance to the river before reaching the South Carolina state line. The landing is on the northwest side of the river, across from the town of Fair Bluff.

The landscape on this 16.6-mile float to the U.S. 76 bridge (B) is mostly forest, with a few houses. The sinuous river creates sandbars at every turn, providing sparkling white beaches that invite stops for picnicking or swimming.

Farther down, a railroad bridge provides a landmark. The U.S. 76 bridge is 45 minutes away from this point.

At U.S. 76, take out on the right (west) side. The Ricefield Cove public landing is about 0.25 mile downstream on the Horry County (east) side. To reach it, go 0.7 miles east on U.S. 76, turn right (south) on an unpaved road.

U.S. 76 to S.C. 917

Below the bridge, the bends become more frequent and pronounced on the 4.8-mile float to the confluence with the Little Pee Dee, which enters from the right.

From the confluence, river houses dominate the Little Pee Dee's banks for much of the remaining 6.3 miles.

There are two intermediate landings. McMillans is on the Marion County (west) side, less than a mile below the confluence. It is 2.0 miles south of U.S. 76 at the Little Pee Dee on S-319.

Red Bluff is about 4.5 miles below the confluence on the same side. From the U.S. 76 bridge, go 0.1 mile west, turn left (south) on S-31, continue 2.3 miles to S-593. Follow S-593 to the landing.

Just below the S.C. 917 bridge, Sandy Bluff Bridge, (C), take out on the left (east) side at Pleasant Hill public landing.

Lumber River at a Glance

Trail: N.C. 904 to S.C. 917 on Little Pee Dee River

Length: 27.7 miles

Topographic Maps: Fair Bluff (NC), Lake View, Nichols

County Maps: Columbus (NC), Dillon, Horry, Marion, Robeson (NC)

Average Flow: Not available

Flood Stage: Not established

Gradient: 25 feet, or 0.9 feet per mile

Difficulty: Flatwater

Hazards: A few logs

Runnable Water Level: Runnable year-round

Suitable For: Beginners

Lynches River

The Lynches River loops through the Sandhills and coastal plain, coursing through pine uplands and bald cypress swamps before flowing into the Great Pee Dee near Johnsonville in Florence County.

Snow Island, Francis Marion's staging area during the Revolutionary War, is bordered in part by the Lynches before it joins the Great Pee Dee River.

A 54-mile stretch of the Lynches has been designated a state Scenic River, the second longest segment in the state. The segment runs from U.S. 15 to Lynches River Regional Park.

The Lynches glides through the truck and tobacco farms of Darlington, Florence, Lee, and Sumter Counties, coursing through extensive swamps on its way. The river rewards those who venture into its swamps. The surroundings are hushed and serene, wildlife is more abundant, and human disturbance is minimal. Be sure to carry a hatchet or saw when paddling through these wilder reaches. Such sections may be too difficult for less-experienced canoeists because of the confusing channels and numerous obstructions.

The current in the Lynches can be zippy when the river level ranges between 4 and 7 feet on the Effingham gauge at the U.S. 52 bridge. Below that level, the going will be strenuous because sunken logs become exposed, requiring frequent haul-outs.

U.S. 15 to Lee State Park

A landing just northeast of Bishopville on U.S. 15 (A) on the left (east) bank of the river is the first good place to start a float trip on the Lynches, simply because the launching is easier. This is the beginning of the designated scenic area. Lee State Park, however, is only 3 miles downstream.

Lee State Park to U.S. 76

This section is 19.8 miles long.

Lee State Park (B) offers several places to launch. The park has a one-way loop road that borders the river for about 0.25 mile.

Spanish moss and native cane mark this section of the trail, 93.5 miles from the confluence with the Great Pee Dee. After passing under I-20, the river slips past pastures and woodlands on its way to U.S. 401, 8.4 miles and three hours downstream. A take-out is on the right (west) side at a public boat landing above the bridge.

Below U.S. 401, the Lynches runs a straighter course between higher, well-defined banks in this 11.4-mile segment. Signs of beaver activity can be seen along the shore. At U.S. 76 (C), take out on the right (west) side between the railroad trestle and the highway bridge. This is the Cartersville public boat landing.

U.S. 76 to U.S. 301

From U.S. 76, it's 16.2 miles to U.S. 301, a journey that takes paddlers through a minefield of river debris in a swamp forest.

This section is broken into two near-equal parts by S.C. 403. Paddlers who don't want to float the entire section can take out at the S.C. 403 bridge. The landing is on the left (east) side about 100 yards below the bridge.

In the 7.1-mile stretch from S.C. 403 to U.S. 301 (D), the channel is relatively clear with few logs blocking the way. Cross vine hangs over the river from low limbs, and bright green duckweed leans with the current.

At U.S. 301, the landing is on the left (north) side below the bridge.

U.S. 301 to Lynches River Regional Park

For the next 11.4 miles, the river channel is clear and passable.

The float time to an alternate take-out, S-55-501, is three hours. The landing is below the bridge on the right (east) side.

Here the river begins a more direct course through pine forest on its way to the park (E), 5.3 miles downstream. Watch for the park's parking lot on the right (east) side. Haul out at the downriver edge of the parking lot.

Lynches River Regional Park to S-46

Boaters can launch at the parking lot or about 3.1 miles downstream at the U.S. 52 bridge, at a public boat landing.

The river continues its run through upland forests, then returns to swamp for the 9.2 miles below U.S. 52 to S-46 (F).

At S-46, the take-out is 50 yards below the bridge on the left (east) side.

S-46 to S-49

Below here, the Lynches takes on the character of a true swamp river. The river loops gracefully past tupelo, red maple, and bald cypress, gurgling as the water ripples through low-hanging branches. This 27.4-mile stretch takes about 16 hours to paddle due to the number of false channels and tight passages. It also appears to be the wildest part of the Lynches, no place for those who wince at the thought of brushing through vines, moss and spiders.

While there is no access at U.S. 378, 6.2 miles away, there are two public boat landings in the area. Lee Landing, off S-461, is about a mile below U.S. 378 just east of the river. The other, Smith, is at the end of S-636 south of its intersection with U.S. 378.

The next take-out is 12.2 miles below U.S. 378 at S-49. Land below the bridge on the right (south) side.

It's another 9.0 miles to S.C. 41-51 (G). A concrete ramp is on the right (south) side below the bridge at the Odell Veuters boat landing.

S.C. 41-51 to Dunham Bluff Landing

This section is not recommended for anyone who is not familiar with the river because of the danger of getting lost. In its 6.4-mile meander to the Great Pee Dee, the Lynches enters a large swamp forest that passes beside Snow Island. The river branches into a number of side channels that are hard to tell from the main channel.

At one point an unmarked channel called "The Cut" veers to the right and joins Clark Creek, which also flows to the Great Pee Dee. You will know you're on Clark Creek if you come to a bridge. The bridge is just beyond the end of S-121, 3.3 miles east of Johnsonville.

To reach Dunham Bluff Landing on the Great Pee Dee, keep bearing to the left on the Lynches. Once on the Great Pee Dee, Dunham Bluff (H) will be 2.5 miles downstream from the confluence. It is on the left (north) side at the end of a dirt road that runs south from the intersection of U.S. 378 and S.C. 908.

Lynches River at a Glance

Trail: Lee State Park to Dunham Bluff Landing on Great Pee Dee River

Length: 93.5 miles

Topographic Maps: Bishopville, Elliott, Florence East, Florence West, Hyman, Johnsonville, Lake City, Lynchburg

County Maps: Darlington, Florence, Lee, Marion

Average Flow: 1,026 cubic feet per second or 27.6 million gallons per hour at U.S. 52 bridge

Flood Stage: 14 feet at U.S. 52 (Effingham)

Gradient: 120 feet, or 1.3 feet per mile

Difficulty: Flat water, deadfalls and logs in most sections

Hazards: False and disappearing channels between U.S. 378 and S.C. 41-51; sandbars and side channels below S.C. 41-51

Runnable Water Level: Runnable year-round; exposed logs may make some sections difficult in low water

Suitable For: Beginners, except for the sections between U.S. 76 and U.S. 301, and between S-46 and the Great Pee Dee

Okatie-Colleton Rivers

The Okatie and Colleton Rivers are really one river with two names. Somewhere around a horseshoe bend between Okatie Bluff and Garretts Point, the Okatie becomes the Colleton. The coastal river widens before merging with the Chechessee River en route to Port Royal Sound.

Although this 6.2-mile river trail is entirely in southeastern Beaufort County near Bluffton and Hilton Head Island, it drains bays, branches, and swamps from adjacent Jasper County.

The Okatie (also spelled Okatee) is named after a tribe of Indians that once prospered in the saltwater marsh environment. Pottery shards and other artifacts have been unearthed as evidence of the Indians that occupied the area from 4,000 years ago until European settlers displaced them.

Trask Landing to S.C. 170

A trip on the Okatie-Colleton means paddling the river backward. Begin at Trask Landing (A), where the river meets the Chechessee, or at S.C. 170 (B). It is no longer possible to access the headwaters of the Okatie from U.S. 278.

You can also inquire about putting in at two private landings, Cherry Point Landing or Camp St. Mary's. Both are off S.C. 170, in the vicinity of Garretts Point, a big loop in the Okatie before it joins with Chechessee Creek (not the Chechessee River) and becomes the Colleton River.

On an incoming tide, you can then paddle upstream to Garretts Point (B) and then return with the outgoing tide to Trask Landing.

Garretts Point makes a good turnaround place, although paddlers can continue farther up the Okatie.

From the headwaters of the Okatie to Pinckney's Colony, a jutting wedge of land about two miles downriver, the river is protected by bluffs and nearby stands of trees. After Pinckney's Colony, the river is bordered by wide expanses of marshlands and tidal flats.

The river, although pristine and scenic, is not isolated from civilization. River houses, from modern designs to the tabby structure of the old Rose Hill Plantation House, dot the banks. A monkey farm was located near here in the 1940s and 1950s. Rhesus monkeys were used in the Salk polio vaccine experiments. Some escaped to nearby sea islands but did not survive.

On the first leg of the horseshoe bend, Camp St. Mary's is on the left (west) side. Now a human development center, it was once a Catholic youth camp.

Half a mile below Garretts Point, a cut branches off to the right and rejoins what becomes the Colleton less than a mile later. When the tide is high, this is an excellent avenue to explore the marshes and to watch fish and shrimp jump in the estuary.

Little channels wend back to the river. A canoe snaking its way through can seem lost to the world in a sea of tall grasses.

The next landmark is Crane Island in the middle of the river. To the left is Callawassie Island where Marlin Perkins of television's *Wild Kingdom* once came to hunt rattlesnakes. The island has been developed as a resort community. Rose Hill Plantation is another mile on the right (west) side.

Sawmill Creek, flowing in from the right, is the last landmark before Trask Landing, a mile upstream from the confluence with the Cheschessee River.

For a side trip on Chechessee Creek, put in at the Edgar Glenn Landing on S.C. 170 (C) on the south side of the bridge. Follow the right bank. The creek mouth is about a mile downstream. The creek follows the contours of Spring Island and Callawassie Island on the west side. It's about 4.0 miles to the connector with the Okatie and another 5.0 miles to Trask Landing.

To make a loop trip, put in at the Edgar Glenn Landing on an outgoing tide, float to the Okatie-Colleton, bear left and take a probe up Callawassie Creek, which has a wider mouth than the two sloughs preceding it. Start your return trip when the tide changes to incoming.

Okatie-Colleton Rivers at a Glance
Trail: Garretts Point to Trask Landing
Length: 6.2 miles
Topographic Map: Jasper
County Map: Beaufort
Average Flow: Not available
Flood Stage: Not established
Gradient: None
Difficulty: Flat tidewater
Hazards: Wind, tides, power boats
Runnable Water Level: Runnable year-round
Suitable For: Beginners accompanied by intermediates

Pocotaligo-Black Rivers

Together, the Pocotaligo and the Black form one of the state's most appealing blackwater river trails, a waterway that wends capriciously through swamp forest in Clarendon, Williamsburg, and Georgetown Counties. The lower 81 miles of the Black have been marked by local paddling enthusiasts and include side trips into the Black River Swamp. A narrow and twisting tributary of the Black, the dark-stained Pocotaligo (pronounced poke-a-TAL-ee-go) joins the larger river about 10 miles below Manning in Clarendon County.

The Black, true to its name, takes on an onyx-like cast as it snakes through the swamp forest of sweet gum, red maple, and river birch along bluffs of loblolly pine and water oak.

The National Park Service surveyed the Black as a possible candidate for the National Wild and Scenic Rivers system. "Southern blackwater stream with limestone bluffs and numerous buttressed tree species; oxbow lakes and white sandbars," the 1982 report read.

Like most rivers, the Black was once used for commercial navigation. Riverboats in the 1700s went up the Black as far as Kingstree, which was a trading center for indigo, flax, and timber. In the 1980s state archeologists recovered part of a sunken 50-foot-long coastal freighter loaded with 10,000 bricks. The freighter, probably on its way to Kingstree, sank 18 miles northwest of Georgetown about 1740.

Wildlife is well represented. Otters live in the Black as far down as S.C. 41 near Andrews. Deer, wood ducks, and even wild hogs can be seen. Alligators prefer the lower stretches.

Plant life includes wild primrose, spider lilies, and yellow-budded water lilies.

A 75.0-mile segment of the Black, from S-40 in Clarendon County to Peahouse Landing at S-38 in Georgetown County, was designated a state scenic river in 2001.

U.S. 301-521 to S-50

This trail begins on the Pocotaligo River at the U.S. 301-521 bridge (A) 1.1 miles north of Manning. Put in on the right (west) side above the bridge at the Pocotaligo Swamp Park.

This 8.8-mile stretch is flanked by swampy terrain on both sides and fed by numerous creeks that may disappear when water levels are down. Lakewood Creek flows in from the left about two miles above the S-50 bridge (B), a mile upriver from the confluence with the Black.

Take out on the right (west) side above the S-50 bridge.

S-50 to S-35

The Pocotaligo joins the Black about a mile below the S-50 bridge. It's 2.5 miles from the confluence to Martin's Lake, a good fishing spot.

The S-35 bridge (C), just inside Williamsburg County, is the last take-out until Gilland Memorial Park Landing above U.S. 52. S-35 has a throw-in with access on either side above the bridge.

S-35 to U.S. 52

This 14.7-mile section moves like a corkscrew, turning numerous times until it reaches the outskirts of Kingstree and Gilland Memorial Park Landing. Like the preceding section, downfalls can be troublesome when water levels are low. Be sure to carry a bush ax or saw.

Gilland Memorial Park Landing is on the left (north) bank. From U.S. 52 in Kingstree, take S-527 north 0.5 miles, turn left (south) and follow the road to the river.

Take out 100 yards above the U.S. 52 bridge (D) on the left (north) side at Mill Street Landing.

U.S. 52 to S-30

Along this 18.5-mile section, the Black is 20 to 30 yards wide. Snags in the middle of the river and overhanging branches are frequent.

A private landing is just below the S-30 bridge, on the left (north) side.

S-30 to S.C. 41

Below the bridge, the Black slows as it widens to about 50 yards. Several houses appear. Then the river constricts to a channel as narrow as 10 yards at some points, resuming its tortuous course through the swamps.

Keep a short watch for the main channel in this swampy 19.7-mile section. It contains oxbow lakes that, when water levels are high, become flooded and resemble the main channel.

Five miles above S.C. 41, houses are sprinkled along the banks.

At the S.C. 41 bridge (F), take out at Pump House Landing, about 200 yards downstream on the right (south) side, off S-303.

S.C. 41 to S.C. 51

The Black broadens during its 23.3-mile trek to S.C. 51.

After the first mile, the river tightens up in an area called "The Narrows," taking paddlers through a labyrinth of trees and bushes before widening again.

Much of the area bordering the eastern side of this stretch of river has been acquired by The Nature Conservancy. The Black River Preserve encompasses 1,276 acres of mostly cypress, tupelo, and gum swamp and features old-growth loblolly hummocks and rare plants such as false dragonhead and riverband quillwort.

Pine Tree Landing is about four hours downstream on the left (north) bank at the end of a dirt road off S-38, 1.7 miles east of S.C. 41.

Pea House public landing is about two hours beyond Pine Tree at the end of S-38, 4.4 miles from S.C. 41.

At. S. C. 51 (G), take out at Browns Ferry public landing on the left (north) side or just before the bridge on the right (south) side. Westvaco maintains a small park with picnic tables and cooking grates here.

S.C. 51 to U.S. 701

The river widens and straightens on this 17.0-mile stretch.

A few plantation houses and outbuildings can be seen along the river. Just beyond the S-179 bridge is Rocky Point public landing on the left (north) side at the end of a dirt road off S-4, 0.9 mile south of S-6.

Take out at the Shrine Club public landing on the right (south) side of the river several hundred yards before the U.S. 701 bridge (H). It is 8.2 miles from the bridge to the confluence with the Great Pee Dee River just above Winyah Bay.

Black River Tributaries

Two creeks that flow into the Black—Black Mingo and Peters—offer a couple of good paddling excursions.

Black Mingo Creek can be accessed from U.S. 41 between Andrews in Georgetown County and Hemingway in Williamsburg County. The float trip is about 10 miles and the creek is fairly open for the most part—not too many tight spots. The creek flows into the Black River about 1.5 miles from Brown's Ferry Landing on S.C. 51. Bear right at the confluence and paddle upstream to get to the landing.

Peters Creek can be accessed on S-4 2.0 miles northwest of U.S. 701 near Georgetown.

photo by Jack Horan

High ground draws paddlers on a swampy section of the Black River.

<u>Pocotaligo-Black Rivers at a Glance</u>

Trail: U.S. 301-501 to U.S. 701

Length: 109.3 miles

Topographic Maps: Andrews, Carvers Bay,
    Georgetown South, Indiantown, Kingstree,
    Manning, Olin, Rhems, Sumter

County Maps: Clarendon, Georgetown,
    Williamsburg

Average Flow: 929 cubic feet per second or 25.0
    million gallons per hour at U.S. 52 bridge

Flood Stage: 12 feet at U.S. 52 (Kingstree)

Gradient: 66 feet, or 0.6 feet per mile

Difficulty: Flatwater

Hazards: Snags, overhanging limbs, strainers,
    particularly in the upper sections

Runnable Water Level: Runnable year-round.
    Exposed logs may make the sections above
    U.S. 52 too difficult in low water.

Suitable For: Beginners accompanied by
    intermediates.

Salkehatchie-Combahee Rivers

The Big Salkehatchie (pronounced SAHL-ketchie by local residents) flows through one of the few remaining primitive blackwater swamps not protected by public ownership in South Carolina. This Lowcountry swamp, before the Big and Little Salkehatchie Rivers merge, shows scarce sign of human intrusion.

The two rivers join to form the Combahee (pronounced CUM-bee), which flows past old rice fields and plantations on its way through coastal marshes to the Atlantic Ocean. The river is part of the ACE (Ashepoo, Combahee, Edisto) Basin.

Below S.C. 63, between Hampton and Colleton Counties, the Big Salkehatchie branches into numerous channels as it courses across a broad cypress swamp, making a canoe float as much a test of pathfinding skills as a pleasure outing.

Over the years, others have found the rivers difficult to ply. Architect Robert Mills in 1825 saw the pair as a candidate for a log-clearing project. "The Combahee ... may be navigable to Barnwell Courthouse by merely removing logs, which now obstruct it," Mills wrote in his *Mills' Atlas of South Carolina*.

Later that century, in 1896, the U.S. Army Corps of Engineers cleared a channel for rafts and flatboats at a cost of $15,840. The 42-mile project, from U.S. 601 south to U.S. 17, remains strewn with logs.

A 1971 survey of the rivers for National Wild and Scenic River system consideration took note of scenic and historic values. "In its lower reaches, the Combahee River swamp is transformed into broad expanses of marshlands and abandoned rice fields, remaining traces of an era existing over a hundred years ago when rice was king and the pace of life moved no faster than boats on this community waterway," the survey said.

Wildlife is plentiful. White ibis, little blue herons, yellow-crowned night herons, osprey, and barred owls live along the rivers. Striped bass, American shad, and Atlantic sturgeon migrate up the lower part of the Combahee.

S.C. 63 to U.S. 17A-21

The 37.2-mile trail begins at the S.C. 63 bridge (A). Paddlers should carry enough food for several days because of the chance of getting lost in this thick swamp.

Follow the left (east) side of the river, although deadfalls and cypress knees will force canoeists to bear to the right at times.

After about three hours—there are few landmarks to measure distance in this 18.8-mile stretch—the braid of channels comes together into a single channel 30 to 40 feet wide. The swamp is almost completely enclosed by a canopy of trees.

The first of two sets of power lines will appear after five hours' paddle. There is almost no high ground in the swamp, except for a spot or two on the east side.

After nine hours, you begin to notice subtle changes in the swamp. The dense canopy opens up, the volume of water seems to increase, and the main channel stands out from the side channels. At this point the confluence with the Little Salkehatchie is an hour away.

The Little Salkehatchie enters from the left above I-95. The U.S. 17A-21 bridge (B) is about an hour and a half from the confluence.

Take out either at a commercial landing on the left (east) side or at a public boat landing on the right (west) side.

U.S. 17A to Sugar Creek Landing

Just below the landings, the Combahee cuts a 25-mile swath through plantation country, changing from a blackwater stream to a brackish-water tidal river. Rice fields dating from the early eighteenth century have reverted to their natural state, providing habitat for waterfowl and other wildlife.

The first landing on this 8.8-mile section is Public Landing, two miles below U.S. 17A-21 on the left (east) side. To reach it, take U.S. 17A-21 east 1.6 miles from the river, turn right (south) at a gravel road.

The Cherokee and Combahee plantations dominate the left (east) side of the river for several miles. On the right (west) side, the first plantation is Auld Brass, which was designed by famed architect Frank Lloyd Wright. Next, in order, are Brewton, Twickenham, and Bonny Hall. Clearly visible from the river is Parker's Ferry where British author Somerset Maugham wrote *The Razor's Edge*.

Sugar Creek Landing (C) is 8.8 miles downstream on the left (west) side. From Yemasee, take S-33 south 6.2 miles to a gravel road and turn left.

Sugar Hill Landing to U.S. 17

Along this 9.6-mile section, from the landing to the U.S. 17 bridge, Steel Bridge (D), the tide becomes a factor. As the river progresses toward St. Helena Sound, cord grass and marshes replace the swamp hardwoods. Wading birds and seabirds are abundant and noisy. In the summer, alligators, turtles, and snakes are common.

Part of the ACE (Ashepoo, Combahee, Edisto) Basin National Wildlife Refuge lies along the river's east side. The tide influences the river here.

About 7.0 miles below Sugar Hill Landing, Cuckhold's Creek enters from the left side. Cuckhold's Creek public boat landing is about 3.5 miles up the creek just below S-66. To get to the landing from U.S. 17A-21, go 5.1 miles east from the Combahee bridge and turn right (south) on S-66. Follow S-66 9.2 miles to the creek.

At Cuckhold's Creek, which runs between the communities of Garden's Corner and Ashepoo, take out at the boat ramp on the right (west) side. Near here, at Tar Bluff on the Combahee, American colonel John Laurens was killed on August 27, 1782, during one of the last battles of the Revolutionary War.

From U.S. 17, it's 20 miles to St. Helena Sound, a trek not recommended for canoeists who don't have nautical charts and a compass.

Salkehatchie-Combahee Rivers at a Glance

Trail: S.C. 63 to U.S. 17

Length: 37.2 miles

Topographic Maps: Cummings, Green Pond,
    Yemassee

County Maps: Beaufort, Colleton, Hampton

Average Flow: 349 cubic feet per second or 9.4
    million gallons per hour at U.S. 601 bridge

Flood Stage: Not established

Gradient: 20 feet, or 0.6 feet per mile

Difficulty: Flatwater

Hazards: Numerous confusing channels; logs and
cypress knees block the channels in the
upper section; little high ground for camping
Runnable Water Level: The section above U.S.
17A-21 can be floated in high water only.
Suitable For: Intermediate and advanced

Santee River

Before the Santee Cooper lakes were impounded in 1942, the Santee River drained the fourth largest watershed in the eastern United States. The Santee, formed at the confluence of the Congaree and Wateree Rivers below Columbia, was dammed to create the 173-square-mile Lake Marion and the 94-square-mile Lake Moultrie. The project diverted water to the Cooper River, reducing the flow of the Santee considerably. Both rivers empty into the Atlantic Ocean between Charleston and Georgetown.

The Santee has once again become the major artery as a result of a U.S. Army Corps of Engineers rediversion project completed in 1985. Its purpose is to reduce silt carried by the Cooper into Charleston Harbor. The rediversion canal runs from Lake Moultrie to the Santee, entering at a point 11.8 miles below the U.S. 52 bridge near St. Stephen.

The Corps says the operation of the St. Stephen hydroplant means the water level of the Santee at U.S. 17A-S.C. 41 will vary between 10.7 and 11.9 feet on weekdays and from 6.3 to 11.3 on weekends. At times when the hydroplant runs at full capacity, the river stage will be about 14.5 feet, sending the Santee out of its banks near the river channel. What the rediversion project means for the canoeist is a slightly quicker current on the lower Santee.

Upstream, the river level is controlled by the Santee Dam at Lake Marion. Releases can run from 5,000 to 40,000 cubic feet per second. To obtain water information, call Santee Cooper at (800) 925-2537 anytime.

The Santee wanders through a broad floodplain forest in its 86.9-mile course to the Atlantic, splitting into the North Santee and the South Santee channels above U.S. 17-701. The river borders privately owned forest land along the upper stretches, from Wilson's Landing to the rediversion canal. Below that, much of the land on the right (west) bank is in the Francis Marion National Forest.

Camping on National Forest land along the river is allowed with a free permit. Permits for the upper half may be obtained from the Witherbee Ranger District office, Box 402, Bethera, S.C. 29430. Phone: (843) 336-3248. Permits for the lower half may be obtained from the Wambaw Ranger District office, Box 106, McClellanville, S.C.

29458. Phone: (843) 887-3311.

The predominantly pine forest provides habitat for deer, turkey, gray fox, and an occasional black bear. The forest has one of the largest populations of red-cockaded woodpeckers in the nation. Swallow-tailed kites and bald eagles are sometimes seen along the Santee, and adjacent creeks and ponds are home to wood ducks, beaver, alligators, crappie, mullet, striped bass, largemouth bass, and redbreast bream.

The Santee was a major waterway during the nineteenth century, with the completion of the Santee Canal in 1800. The 22-mile-long canal connected the Santee to the Cooper River near Moncks Corner, providing a shortcut from the Upcountry to Charleston. The toll canal closed in 1850.

Wilson's Landing to U.S. 52

The first launching site below Lake Marion is Wilson's Landing (A), a public landing at the end of S-31.

This portion of the river is Francis Marion country. The Revolutionary War hero known as the Swamp Fox is buried on the southern fringe of the Santee Swamp beneath live oaks near Belle Isle Plantation. Signs along S.C. 45 direct the traveler to Marion's tomb and the remnants of the Santee Canal.

This part of the river is more sinuous than the lower sections, making a twisting 23.2-mile journey to the U.S. 52 (B) bridge. The trip takes six to seven hours.

Take out on the left (north) side just below the bridge at the U.S. 52 public landing.

U.S. 52 to Laurel Hill Landing

The next section is a 14.8-mile run to Lauren Hill Landing (C), a public landing near Alvin in Berkeley County.

The first landmark on the river, 4.8 miles downstream, is a railroad trestle, followed 7.0 miles farther by the rediversion canal on the right.

Arrowhead Landing is on the rediversion canal 2.0 miles southeast of St. Stephen. It can be reached by taking S.C. 45 through St. Stephen and turning left at a sign advertising a tackle shop. It's 0.8 miles to the ramp, which is about 0.5 mile down the canal to the river.

From Arrowhead, it's three miles to the Laurel Hill Landing on the right (south) side. The landing is located on Forest Service Road 144 5.0 miles southeast of St. Stephen.

Laurel Hill Landing to U.S. 17A-S.C. 41

The distance from Laurel Hill Landing to U.S. 17A-S.C. 41 (D) is 12.6 miles. Take out on the right (south) side below the bridge at Leneuds Ferry Landing.

U.S. 17A-S.C. 41 to McConnell's Landing

This stretch has long straightaways and a few horseshoe bends. Moderate bluffs guard the right bank, and a floodplain swamp borders the left bank.

One of the bluffs is the site of a Civil War battery manned by Confederate artillery. The battery commanded a good view of the river in both directions. An alert paddler might be able to spot the site, about a mile upriver from McConnell's Landing. It may also be reached by foot from the end of Forest Service Road 204D.

The Santee widens to about 100 feet from U.S. 17-S.C. 41 near Jamestown. The current begins to feel a slight influence from tides at this point.

It's 11.4 miles from U.S. 17A-S.C. 41 to McConnell's Landing (E), a concrete ramp that is also called Pleasant Hill Landing, on the right (south) side.

To paddle to Guillard Lake Scenic Area in the National Forest, locate a hand-dug canal that was built by slave labor. It is about 5.0 miles downriver from Leneuds Ferry Landing on the right. The scenic area is less than 0.25 mile away on the left side of the oxbow lake, marked by a bluff.

To get to McConnell's Landing, take S.C. 45 from Jamestown 7.5 miles and turn left (north) just past Echaw Creek on S-103. At Forest Service Road 204, turn left again 1.6 miles from the first turnoff. At the Waterhorn Hunt Unit entrance (4.6 miles), bear left on Forest Service Road 204F. The landing is 1.6 miles.

McConnell's Landing to Collins Landing

Below McConnell's Landing, the Santee splits into the North Santee and South Santee. This trail follows the North Santee, which has two access points.

To avoid confusion at Goat Island, 6.3 miles away, carry a compass and a Forest Service map of the river. A boater who accidentally goes down the South Santee can continue the 2.4 miles to the mouth of Wambaw Creek and paddle 2.1 miles up the creek to Forest Service Road 204.

To follow the North Santee, bear to the left on the channel that connects the Santee with Wadmacon Creek. Once on the North Santee, Collins public landing (F) is on the left (north) side in Georgetown County 2.6 miles below the beginning of Goat Island.

From U.S. 17-701 at the Santee, go 2.8 miles north to S-24, turn left (west) and go 2.9 miles to a dirt road and turn left. Follow the road to the river.

Collins Landing to U.S. 17-701

The public landing at U.S. 17-701 (G) is 3.2 miles away. Take out on the left (north) side below the bridge.

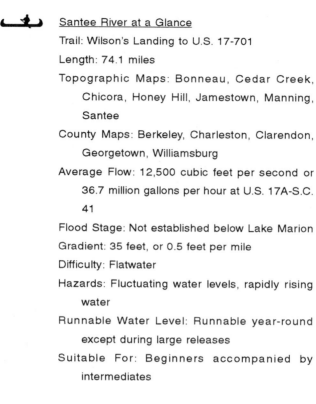

Santee River at a Glance

Trail: Wilson's Landing to U.S. 17-701

Length: 74.1 miles

Topographic Maps: Bonneau, Cedar Creek, Chicora, Honey Hill, Jamestown, Manning, Santee

County Maps: Berkeley, Charleston, Clarendon, Georgetown, Williamsburg

Average Flow: 12,500 cubic feet per second or 36.7 million gallons per hour at U.S. 17A-S.C. 41

Flood Stage: Not established below Lake Marion

Gradient: 35 feet, or 0.5 feet per mile

Difficulty: Flatwater

Hazards: Fluctuating water levels, rapidly rising water

Runnable Water Level: Runnable year-round except during large releases

Suitable For: Beginners accompanied by intermediates

Waccamaw River

The Waccamaw, South Carolina's easternmost river, begins in the waters of Lake Waccamaw, a natural lake in Columbus County, North Carolina.

The lake and the river draw their name from the Waccamaw Indian tribe, which lived in the area in small settlements when the Europeans arrived in the 1600s. Pronounced WAH-kam-aw, the river parallels the coast as it makes a 140-mile journey from North Carolina to Winyah Bay at Georgetown.

Since 1880 the U.S. Army Corps of Engineers has been authorized to keep a channel open for commerce from Lake Waccamaw to Georgetown. The Corps completed a channel-clearing project in 1931 and, as recently as 1977, removed snags from Sessions Landing to Conway.

The 56.1-mile trail starts at the N.C. 904 bridge (A), the first put-in, which is above the South Carolina state line. The bridge is 0.7 mile west of the N.C. 905 intersection, 8.5 miles north of Longs, S.C. Put in at the landing on the left (east) side of the river, just below the bridge. The river is about 35 yards wide here but shrinks to around 50 feet wide approximately 3.0 miles downstream.

Along the 16.5-mile section to S.C. 9 (B), the Waccamaw moves like a spiral, looping continuously. The seemingly endless bends make the going slow, so allow more time for a Waccamaw trip.

Beginning at the South Carolina state line, much of the river is bordered by the Waccamaw River Heritage Preserve. The public lands extend to S.C. 31 and are open to riverbank camping.

About 11.0 miles downstream is an alternate take-out at Wortham's Ferry, marked by a high bluff and a sharp right turn in the river. To get to the landing from S.C. 9, take S-57 north 2.3 miles, turn left (west) at S-11 and follow a dirt road to the river.

At the S.C. 9 bridge, take out at the landing on the right (west) side just before the bridge.

S.C. 9 to S-31

From the S.C. 9 bridge, the S-31 bridge (C) is about six hours downstream. The river continues to meander, tightening now and then and picking up a little speed on this 15.1-mile section.

At the S-31 bridge are two take-outs. One is the Red Bluff No. 2 public landing off S. C. 905 above the bridge. The other is on the left (east) side below the bridge.

S-31 to S-105

The Waccamaw departs from its winding ways in this 7.5-mile section, widening and straightening out for most of the way to Conway. Saw palmettos and Spanish moss accent the forest. Bluffs loom over parts of the river.

Take out at the S-105 bridge (D). The Reaves Ferry Public Landing is on the right (west) side of the river.

S-105 to U.S. 501

Below S-105, the river swings toward the west before resuming its southerly course near Conway. The paddler will lose the tug of the current in this 17.0-mile stretch as the river widens and deepens. As the river turns south, the Savannah Bluff public landing appears on the right (east) side at Conway, just beyond the U.S. 501 bypass bridge (E).

Waccamaw River at a Glance
Trail: N.C. 904 to U.S. 501 Bypass
Length: 56.1 miles
Topographic Maps: Calabash (NC), Conway

Longs: Nixonville, Pireway (NC)

County Maps: Brunswick (NC), Columbus (NC),
   Horry

Average Flow: 1,217 cubic feet per second or
   32.8 million gallons per hour at S.C. 9

Flood Stage: 7 feet at Conway Marina

Gradient: 10 feet, or 0.2 feet per mile

Difficulty: Flatwater

Hazards: Some logs

Runnable Water Level: Runnable year-round

Suitable For: Beginners

Wambaw Creek

Wambaw Creek offers an easy, half-day float along one of coastal South Carolina's five federally designated wilderness areas. The tide-influenced creek, a tributary of the Santee River, heads up into the wetlands of the Francis Marion National Forest in Charleston County.

Though now a protected wilderness, Wambaw Creek has a history of exploitation for rice and timber. Settlers in the 1700s converted parts of the swamp to rice fields. Paddlers can still see remains of the long-abandoned rice field dikes and canals along the creek.

Loggers floated trees down the creek until the late 1800s when large timber companies logged off mature trees from 1885 through 1930, using steam locomotives. The 1,900-acre Wambaw Creek Wilderness was designated in 1980.

The predominantly loblolly and long-leaf pine forest was devastated by Hurricane Hugo in 1989. Visitors may see the rare swallow-tailed kite, red-shouldered hawk, and black-crowned night heron.

S.C. 45 to Still Landing

The 8.7-mile trail begins at the S.C. 45 bridge (A), which is 6.5 miles north of U.S. 17-701. Put in here only in wet months when the flow of water appears ample and the tide is high. Add 4.5 hours to the high tide at Charleston. Otherwise, in low water you'll be clambering over logs and cypress knees during the first 2.0 miles of this 4.7-mile section.

An alternate put-in is at the end of Forest Service Road 212-A. The creek is a short walk.

After two miles, the creek widens into a defined channel of about 25 yards wide.

To locate Still Landing (B), watch for a low bluff on the right (south) side of the creek about a half mile upstream of the concrete ramp. Still Landing is at the end of Forest Service Road 211-B.

Still Landing to Road 204

The Creek follows a series of gentle bends for the remaining 4.0 miles, past large cypress trees and saw palmettos. Flowering plants such as cross vine and golden club add beauty to the creek in spring.

Take out at the public landing on the left (north) side of the creek, just below the Road 204 bridge (C).

The Santee River confluence is 2.1 miles away. There are no more public landings downstream.

Solo canoeist plies Wambaw Creek, a designated federal wilderness area.

Wambaw Creek at a Glance

Trail: S.C. 45 to Forest Service Road 204

Length: 8.7 miles

Topographic Maps: Honey Hill, Santee

County Maps: Berkeley, Charleston

Average Flow: Not available

Flood Stage: Not established

Gradient: None

Difficulty: Flatwater

Hazards: Numerous logs in the first two miles; the
river is influenced by tides

Runnable Water Level: The first few miles may
not be floatable in dry months or at low tide.

Suitable For: Beginners

photo by Jack Horan

Paddlers explore Sparkleberry Swamp, a 16,000-acre floodplain forest east of the
Santee River above Lake Marion.

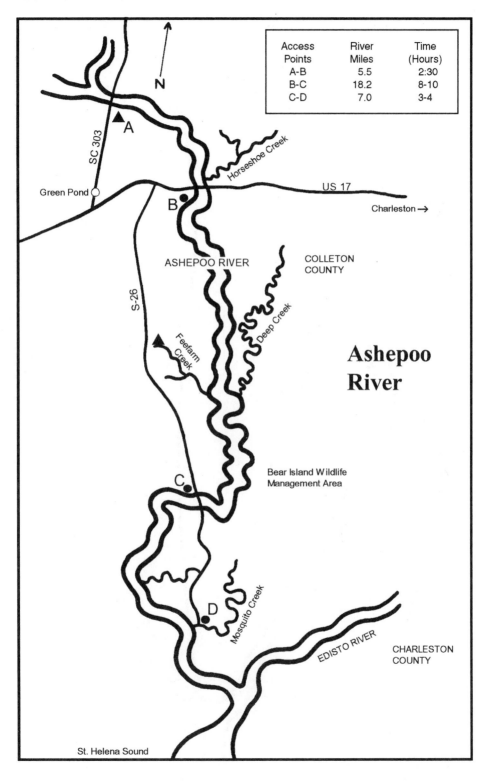

Access Points	River Miles	Time (Hours)
A-B	5.5	2:30
B-C	18.2	8-10
C-D	7.0	3-4

N

SC 303

A

Horseshoe Creek

Green Pond

US 17

B

Charleston →

ASHEPOO RIVER

COLLETON COUNTY

S-26

Deep Creek

Feefarm Creek

Ashepoo River

Bear Island Wildlife Management Area

C

D

Mosquito Creek

EDISTO RIVER

CHARLESTON COUNTY

St. Helena Sound

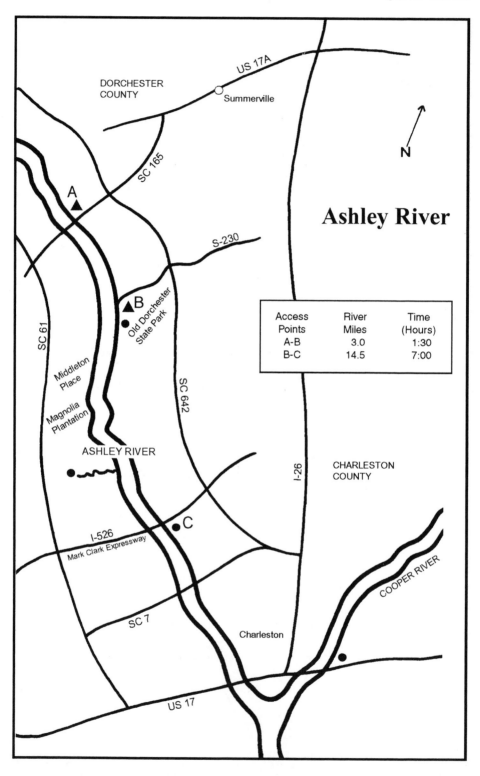

DORCHESTER
COUNTY

US 17A

Summerville

SC 165

N

A

Ashley River

S-230

B
Old Dorchester
State Park

SC 61

Middleton
Place

Magnolia
Plantation

SC 642

ASHLEY RIVER

Access Points	River Miles	Time (Hours)
A-B	3.0	1:30
B-C	14.5	7:00

I-26

CHARLESTON
COUNTY

C

I-526
Mark Clark Expressway

COOPER RIVER

SC 7

Charleston

US 17

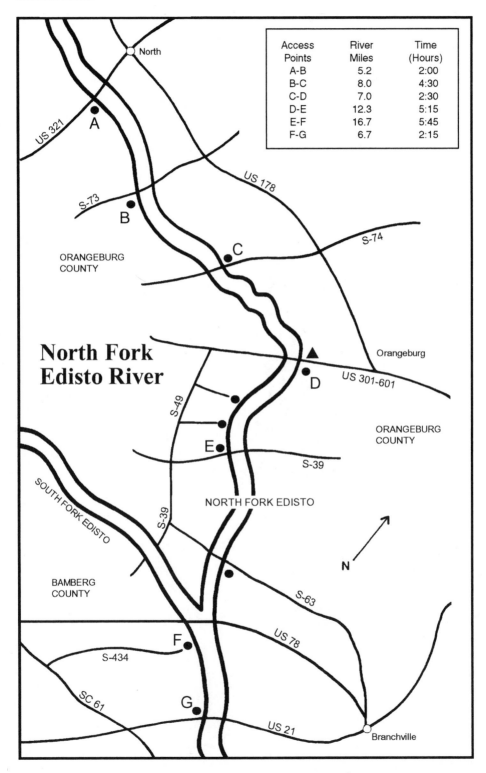

Access Points	River Miles	Time (Hours)
A-B	5.2	2:00
B-C	8.0	4:30
C-D	7.0	2:30
D-E	12.3	5:15
E-F	16.7	5:45
F-G	6.7	2:15

North

US 321

A

US 178

S-73

B

S-74

ORANGEBURG COUNTY

C

North Fork
Edisto River

Orangeburg

D

US 301-601

S-49

ORANGEBURG COUNTY

E

S-39

SOUTH FORK EDISTO

S-39

NORTH FORK EDISTO

N

BAMBERG COUNTY

S-63

F

US 78

S-434

SC 61

G

US 21

Branchville

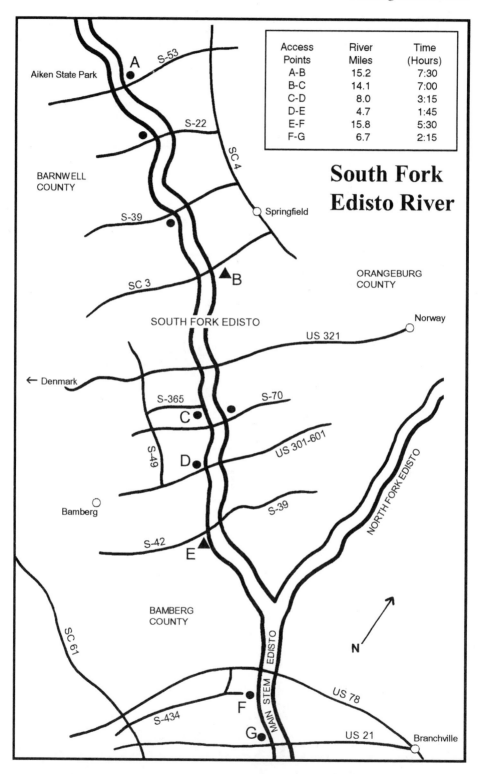

Access	River	Time
Points	Miles	(Hours)
A-B	15.2	7:30
B-C	14.1	7:00
C-D	8.0	3:15
D-E	4.7	1:45
E-F	15.8	5:30
F-G	6.7	2:15

South Fork Edisto River

Aiken State Park

S-53

A

S-22

SC 4

BARNWELL COUNTY

Springfield

S-39

SC 3

B

SOUTH FORK EDISTO

ORANGEBURG COUNTY

Norway

US 321

← Denmark

S-365

S-70

C

S-49

D

US 301-601

NORTH FORK EDISTO

Bamberg

S-39

S-42

E

BAMBERG COUNTY

N

SC 61

EDISTO

MAIN STEM

US 78

F

S-434

G

US 21

Branchville

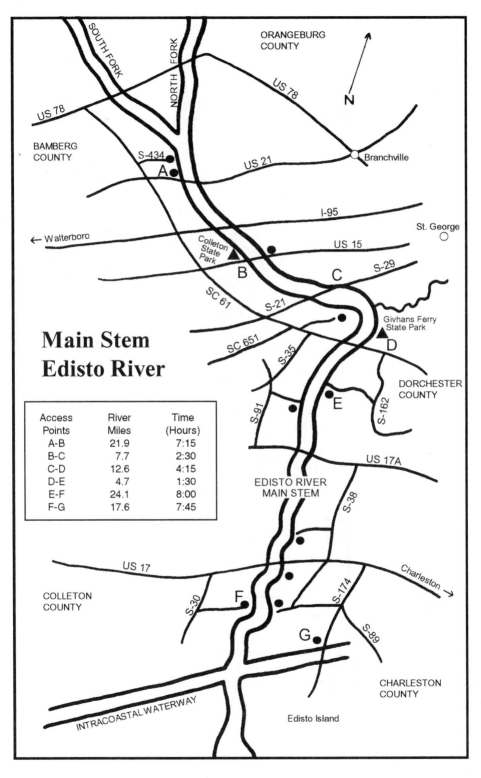

Main Stem Edisto River

Access Points	River Miles	Time (Hours)
A-B	21.9	7:15
B-C	7.7	2:30
C-D	12.6	4:15
D-E	4.7	1:30
E-F	24.1	8:00
F-G	17.6	7:45

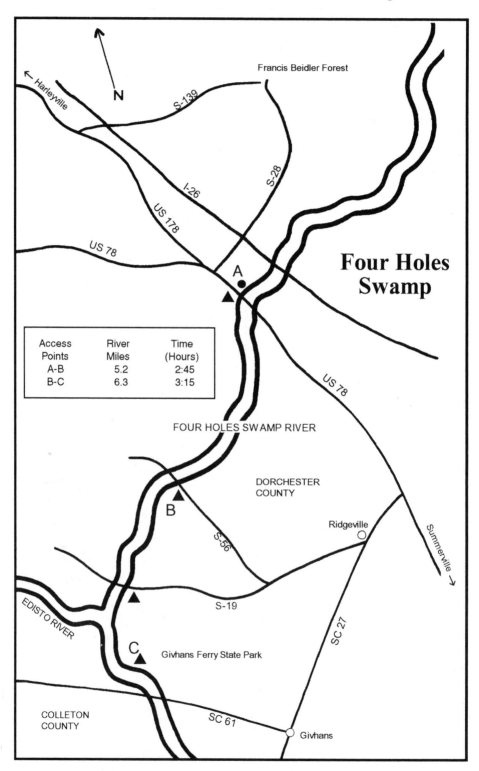

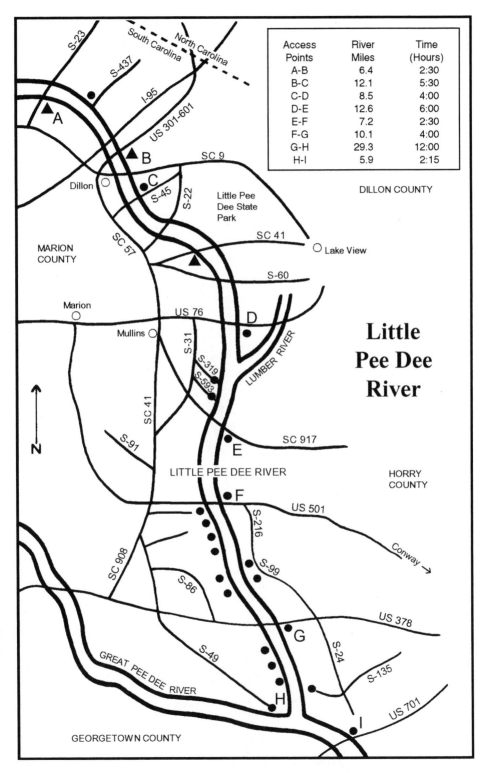

Access Points	River Miles	Time (Hours)
A-B	6.4	2:30
B-C	12.1	5:30
C-D	8.5	4:00
D-E	12.6	6:00
E-F	7.2	2:30
F-G	10.1	4:00
G-H	29.3	12:00
H-I	5.9	2:15

DILLON COUNTY

Little Pee Dee River

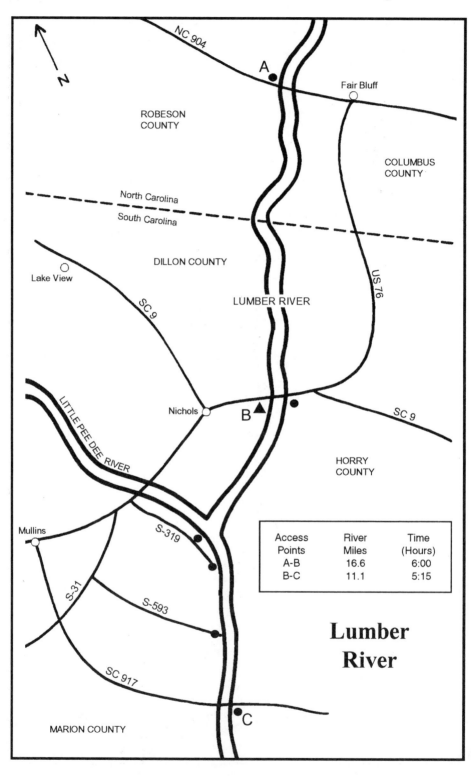

Access Points	River Miles	Time (Hours)
A-B	16.6	6:00
B-C	11.1	5:15

Lumber River

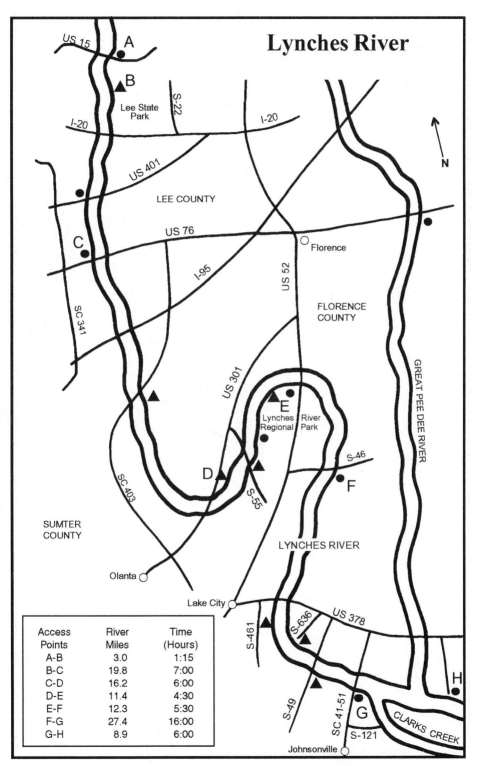

Lynches River

Access Points	River Miles	Time (Hours)
A-B	3.0	1:15
B-C	19.8	7:00
C-D	16.2	6:00
D-E	11.4	4:30
E-F	12.3	5:30
F-G	27.4	16:00
G-H	8.9	6:00

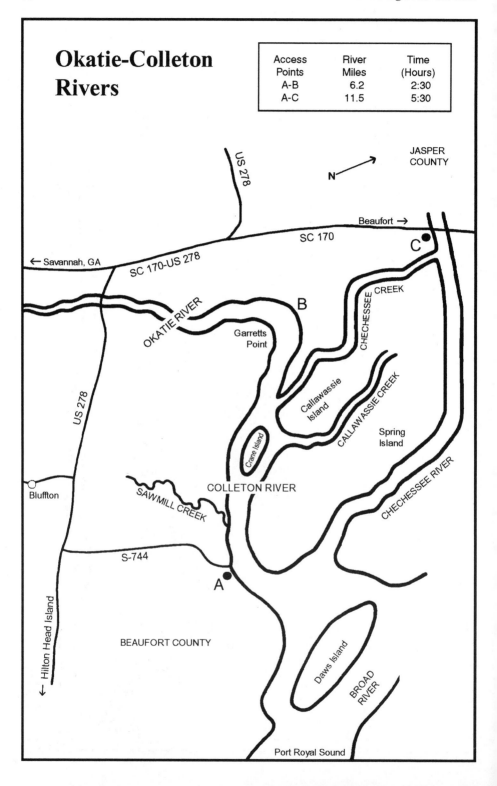

Okatie-Colleton Rivers

Access Points	River Miles	Time (Hours)
A-B	6.2	2:30
A-C	11.5	5:30

US 278

N

JASPER COUNTY

Beaufort →

SC 170

← Savannah, GA

SC 170-US 278

C

CHECHESSEE CREEK

OKATIE RIVER

B

Garretts Point

Callawassie Island

CALLAWASSIE CREEK

Spring Island

US 278

Crane Island

CHECHESSEE RIVER

Bluffton

SAWMILL CREEK

COLLETON RIVER

S-744

A

Hilton Head Island

BEAUFORT COUNTY

Daws Island

BROAD RIVER

Port Royal Sound

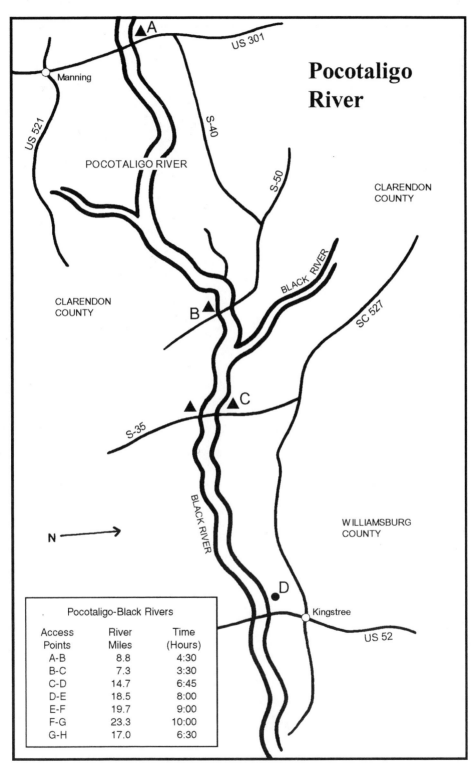

Pocotaligo River

US 301

Manning

US 521

S-40

POCOTALIGO RIVER

S-50

CLARENDON COUNTY

BLACK RIVER

SC 527

CLARENDON COUNTY

B

C

S-35

N →

BLACK RIVER

WILLIAMSBURG COUNTY

D

Kingstree

US 52

Pocotaligo-Black Rivers		
Access Points	River Miles	Time (Hours)
A-B	8.8	4:30
B-C	7.3	3:30
C-D	14.7	6:45
D-E	18.5	8:00
E-F	19.7	9:00
F-G	23.3	10:00
G-H	17.0	6:30

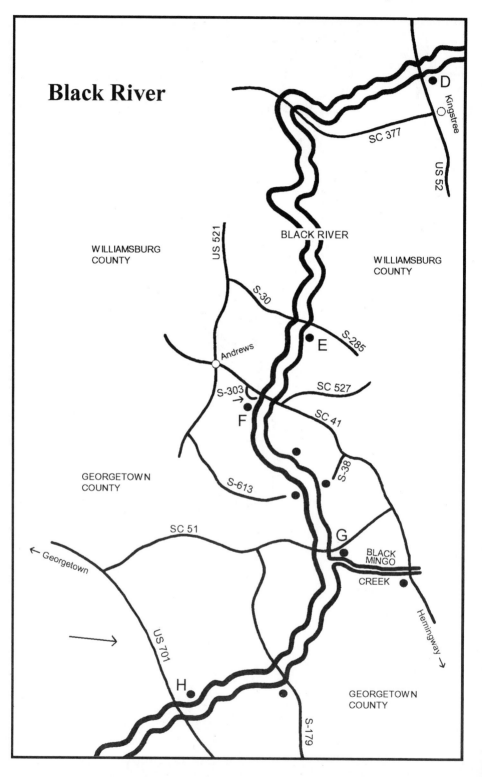

Black River

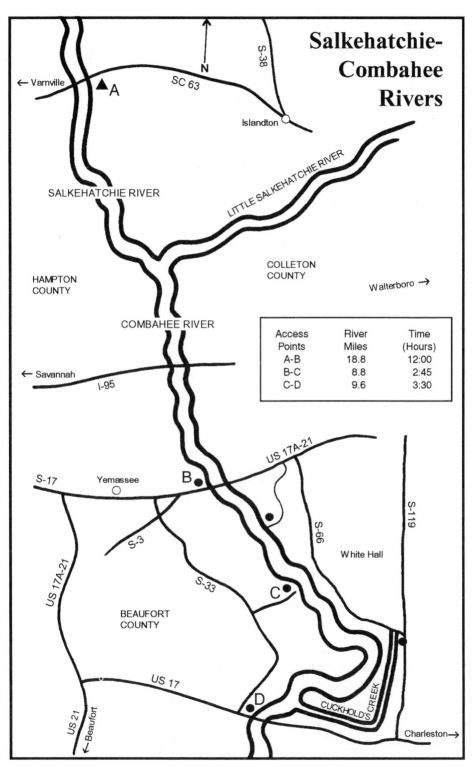

Salkehatchie-Combahee Rivers

Access Points	River Miles	Time (Hours)
A-B	18.8	12:00
B-C	8.8	2:45
C-D	9.6	3:30

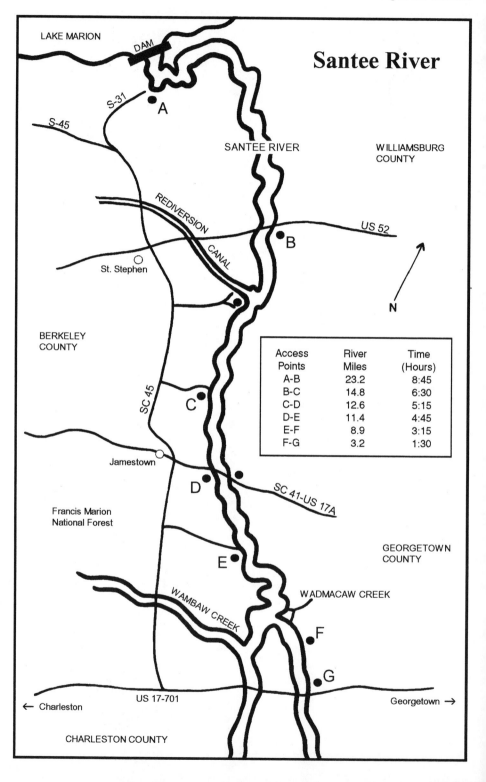

LAKE MARION

DAM

S-31

A

S-45

SANTEE RIVER

WILLIAMSBURG
COUNTY

REDIVERSION

US 52

CANAL

St. Stephen

N

BERKELEY
COUNTY

SC 45

C

Access Points	River Miles	Time (Hours)
A-B	23.2	8:45
B-C	14.8	6:30
C-D	12.6	5:15
D-E	11.4	4:45
E-F	8.9	3:15
F-G	3.2	1:30

Jamestown

B

D

SC 41-US 17A

Francis Marion
National Forest

GEORGETOWN
COUNTY

E

WAMBAW CREEK

WADMACAW CREEK

F

G

US 17-701

← Charleston

Georgetown →

CHARLESTON COUNTY

Santee River

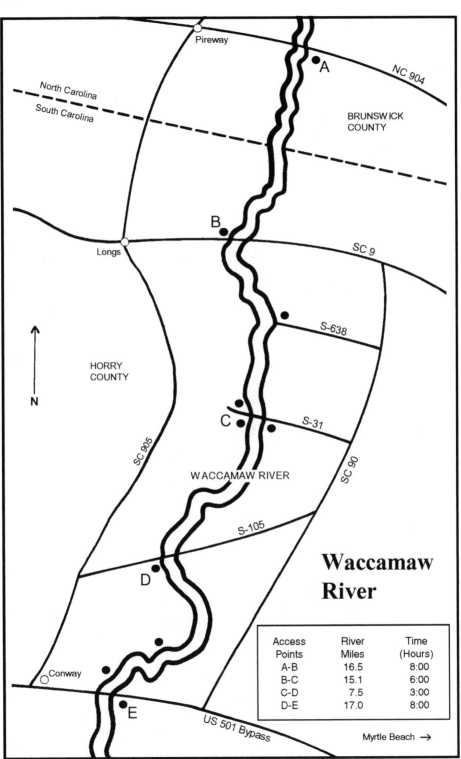

Pireway

North Carolina

South Carolina

NC 904

BRUNSWICK
COUNTY

B

Longs

SC 9

S-638

HORRY
COUNTY

N

SC 905

C

S-31

SC 90

WACCAMAW RIVER

S-105

D

**Waccamaw
River**

Conway

E

US 501 Bypass

Myrtle Beach →

Access Points	River Miles	Time (Hours)
A-B	16.5	8:00
B-C	15.1	6:00
C-D	7.5	3:00
D-E	17.0	8:00

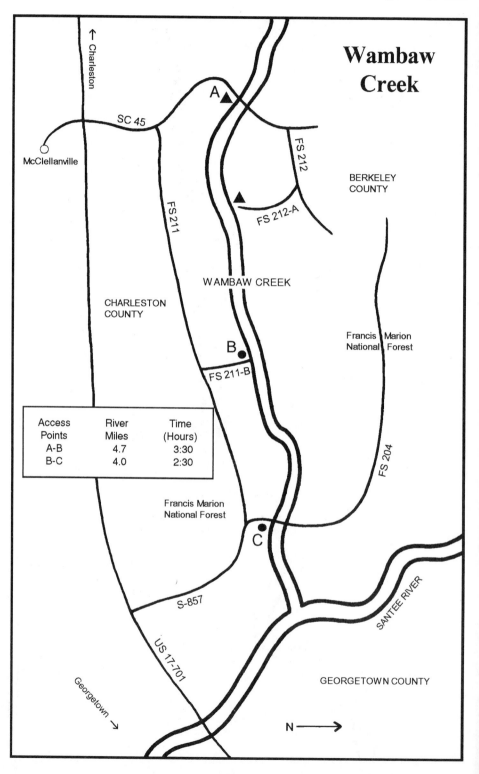

Wambaw Creek

↑ Charleston

SC 45

FS 212

BERKELEY
COUNTY

McClellanville

FS 211

FS 212-A

WAMBAW CREEK

CHARLESTON
COUNTY

Francis Marion
National Forest

B

FS 211-B

Access Points	River Miles	Time (Hours)
A-B	4.7	3:30
B-C	4.0	2:30

FS 204

Francis Marion
National Forest

C

S-857

US 17-701

Georgetown ↘

SANTEE RIVER

GEORGETOWN COUNTY

N ⟶

Piedmont and Midlands Rivers

Broad
Catawba
Congaree
Congaree Swamp
Enoree

Saluda
Turkey-Stevens Creeks
Tyger
Wateree

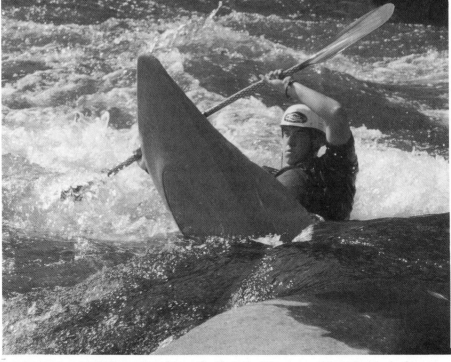

photo by Jack Horan

Section below Mill Race Rapid on the Saluda River provides play hole for kayakers.

Broad River

Spilling out of the western North Carolina mountains, the Broad courses through the Upstate on its way to a rendezvous with the Congaree at Columbia.

The river was once a boundary between claimed lands of the Cherokee and Catawba Indian tribes. Legend says the Cherokees and the Catawbas fought a great battle over the prime hunting grounds between the Broad and the Catawba River to the east. After a truce, the tribes decided the area populated with bison, elk, and deer would be neutral territory.

The Broad drops 380 feet from N.C. 150 in Cleveland County, North Carolina, to S.C. 34 in Fairfield County, the beginning and ending points of this 73.9-mile trail. Five hydroelectric plants along the way tap the power of the falling water.

The Broad's scenery varies from farmland and pasture to the pine and hardwood forests of the Sumter National Forest and private woods.

An 80-mile section below the Gaston Shoals dam contains smallmouth bass, stocked by the state since 1985.

N.C. 150 to S.C. 18

The first put-in above the South Carolina state line is at the Broad River Greenway (A) east of the N.C. 150 bridge.

The upper part of this 8.7-mile section consists of riffles and flatwater.

The Big Bay Access Area on the right (west) side if 0.7 miles above the Gaston Shoals Dam. When approaching Gaston Shoals, watch for a warning sign for the Duke Power Company dam built in 1906. Head for a pier to the left of the dam, the beginning of a 250-yard portage trail that is part of the Broad River Canoe Trail.

Below the dam, the river contains numerous shoals and sandbars. After 1.5 miles, take out on the left (east) side just before the S.C. 18 bridge (B).

S.C. 18 to Ninety-Nine Islands Dam

The Broad passes under the S.C. 18, I-85, and U.S. 29 bridges before arriving at the backwater of the Cherokee Falls Dam in this 8.5-mile section. Approach the dam cautiously. Portage on the right side on the rocks.

After a series of shoals and islands, the river flattens out in the backwater of Ninety-Nine Islands Dam (C), also owned by Duke Power. Keep to the left as the river curves to the right. The dam won't be visible when you take out at the left bend, the Pick Hill Access Area. Don't paddle toward the 70-foot-high dam—two fishermen were swept over it in 1983; one died.

The section from Ninety-Nine Islands Dam to the Pacolet River is a state Scenic River.

Ninety-Nine Islands Dam to Lockhart Dam

Put in at the landing on the left (east) side of the river at the end of S-43 in Cherokee County. The Ninety-Nine Islands Access Area is on the right (west) side at the end of S-13 in Cherokee County.

The next access, Lockhart Dam (D) is 20.8 miles away. The section begins with springy riffles and mild Class I rapids that continue for the first 3.0 or so miles. The S.C. 211 bridge is about 2 hours downstream.

Beyond S.C. 211, the Broad is flatwater most of the way to Lockhart Dam. Watch for a warning sign on the right (west) bank above the dam. Take out here. A call box is located on a small concrete building. When possible, Lockhart Power Company will help boaters portage the dam by hauling their craft on a truck to a downriver access point.

Parking is available at the dam site. To reach it from S.C. 49 at Lockhart, take S-10 north a block to S-308, turn right and go a block to S-31. Follow S-31 for 0.2 miles to the dam.

Lockhart Dam to Sandy River Access Area

Since 1921 virtually all the water in a 1.7-mile stretch of the Broad was diverted through a canal built in the early 1820s to generate electricity by Lockhart Power. That diversion ended in 2000 by agreement between Lockhart, the S.C. Department of Natural Resources, and the U.S. Fish and Wildlife Service, which was approved by the Federal Energy Regulatory Commission. Now, a minimal flow of water continues through the riverbed below S.C. 49 but not enough for paddling.

Two put-ins are 5.0 miles downstream. They are the Broad River and Woods Ferry recreation areas in the Sumter National Forest. Broad River, on the west side in Union County, is off S-86. Take Forest Service Road 312B east 1.0 mile. Woods Ferry, on the east side in Chester County, is off S-49. Take Forest Service Road 574 and follow it 3.6 miles.

The 16.6-mile float to Neal Shoals Dam is primarily flatwater with a few riffles. A designated canoe portage marked by a sign is on the east (left) side of the river before the dam. The first part of the trail comes out on Forest Service Road 304 and then follows an old road bed to the base of the dam.

The last landmark before the Sandy River Access Area (E) is the S.C. 72-121 bridge, which has no access. This bridge is the site of an old Catawba Indian fish dam and a Revolutionary War battle. On November 9, 1780, British mounted troops led by Maj. James Wemyss attacked American general Thomas Sumter's camp before dawn. Sumter's troops, however, won the Battle of Fishdam Ford.

Sandy River comes in from the left (east) side. The landing is just around the bend of the confluence. From S.C. 72-121, follow Forest Service Road 406 to the access.

Sandy River Access Area to S.C. 34

This is the liveliest part of the Broad. The paddling is bouncy but not difficult.

The first landmark on this 15.8-mile segment is Shelton Island, an hour downstream. Take the right channel.

Next is Henderson Island, part of the Henderson Island Scenic Area. An unusual, 35-acre stand of hardwoods covers a steep cove on the right (west) bank. Take the left channel.

For the S.C. 34 bridge (F) access, go about 50 yards below the bridge to a landing on the left (east) bank, the Fairfield County side. To get to the landing from S.C. 34, take a paved road just east of the bridge.

Beyond this point, the Broad enters the backwater of Parr Reservoir, formed by Parr Shoals Dam 10.7 miles away.

Broad River at a Glance

Trail: N.C. 150 to S.C. 34

Length: 73.9 miles

Topographic Maps: Blacksburg-North (NC), Blacksburg-South, Blair, Carlisle, Hickory Grove, Kings Creek, Leeds, Lockhart, Sharon

County Maps: Cherokee, Chester, Cleveland (NC), Fairfield, Newberry, Union, York

Average Flow: 4,041 cubic feet per second or 108.8 million gallons per hour at Carlisle

Flood Stages: 10 feet at U.S. 29 (Gaffney), 14 feet near S.C. 34 bridge (Blair)

Gradient: 380 feet or 5.1 feet per mile

Hazards: Five dams that must be portaged

Difficulty: Flatwater, fast flatwater, Class I rapids

Runnable Water Level: Runnable year-round

Suitable For: Beginners

Catawba River

The workhorse of Carolina rivers, the Catawba powers hydroelectric plants, cools nuclear plants, and provides water for cities and industries as it flows from the North Carolina mountains to the Wateree River.

The river's name comes from "katapa," a Cherokee Indian word for divided, as the upper part of the river in South Carolina was the dividing line between the territories of the Cherokee and the Catawba tribes. Other accounts give the name of the Catawba tribe, and the river, as derived from "Kadapau" and "Kadapahaw."

The Catawba becomes the Wateree River at Lake Wateree near Camden, then merges with the Congaree to form the Santee River.

Around 1820, the Catawba became part of a plan to connect Charleston and the Mississippi River by a series of water routes. The idea was to build canals and locks on the Catawba and Wateree to carry flatboat barges around the rivers' rocky shoals. The river traffic would end near Morganton, North Carolina, where the goods would be loaded onto wagons, hauled across the mountains to the French Broad River near Asheville and then floated to the Tennessee River and on to the Mississippi.

Four canal-lock systems were built in South Carolina but the plan was never completed. Only one canal-lock, built in 1823, remains. The Landsford Canal is preserved at Landsford Canal State Park near Rock Hill.

This 31.7-mile trail from Lake Wylie Dam to S.C. 9, tracks the longest remaining free-flowing section of the Catawba. It's a river worth exploring. The banks have remained largely free of development. Count on seeing birds from osprey and bald eagles (in winter) to great blue herons and cormorants. Largemouth bass, striped bass, and catfish swim the river.

Timing is the key to paddling the Catawba. Without releases from the Lake Wylie Dam, the level of the river is too low to avoid rocks and several long successions of rocky shoals. The on-and-off releases are dictated by electricity demand. The most frequent releases occur in winter, when Duke is moving water downstream to make room in its lakes for spring rains. Scheduled releases are planned. See page 151.

Releases can mean swift currents and big standing waves. Operating two of the four turbines, for example, will raise the water by 3 feet, 200 yards below the dam.

Lake Wylie Dam to River Park

The first section, 6.1 miles, begins at the Fort Mill Access Area (A) below the dam in York County. The access area, about 10 miles south of Charlotte, is between

Tega Cay and I-77, off S.C. 49.

The river begins with mostly flatwater until a small set of rapids appears just before the I-77 bridge. Below U.S. 21, more Class I rapids liven the float. Take out on the right (south) side at the River Park canoe launch (B).

River Park to S.C. 5

The Catawba Indian Reservation is about 10 miles downriver on this 12.3-mile section, along the right (west) bank.

Sugar Creek enters from the left (north) side just before the Catawba takes a turn south. At the bend is a long set of shoals bordered by a steep bluff. Be aware that Class II rapids, strong currents, and standing waves form in high water.

The S.C. 5 bridge (C) is the next take-out. The informal access area on the right (west) side has been closed by the landowner. On the left (east) side, below the bridge, is a path that leads from the river.

photo by Jack Horan

Swift current propels paddlers down the Catawba River.

S.C. 5 to Landsford Canal State Park

Landsford Canal State Park (D) is 3.9 miles away on the right (east) side of the river.

After an island splits the river into two channels, move to the right channel. You will hear the roar of the water rushing through the shoals by this time. The park's low banks provide an easy take-out.

The park has picnic tables, restrooms and a 1.25-mile nature trail that follows the canal and its granite locks.

Landsford Canal State Park to S.C. 9

From the park, stay in the right channel until the end of the island. Cross to the left to take advantage of a greater water flow in the shoals. The shoals can be dangerous. At high water levels, the rapids may approach Class II or III.

Several more islands dot the river in this 7.4-mile section, where the rare Rocky Shoals Spider Lily blooms in late May and early June.

The float concludes at the S.C. 9 bridge (E), where the backwaters of Fishing Creek Lake begin. Take out at the S.C. 9 public landing on the left (Lancaster County) side of the river.

Catawba River at a Glance

Trail: Lake Wylie Dam to S.C. 9

Length: 31.7 miles

Topographic Maps: Catawba, Catawba-Northeast;
    Charlotte (NC), Clover, Lancaster, Rock Hill-
    East, Van Wyck

County Maps: Chester, Lancaster, York.

Average Flow: 4,554 cubic feet per second or
    122.4 million gallons per hour

Flood Stage: Not established

Gradient: 80 feet or 2.5 feet per mile

Difficulty: Fast flatwater, Class I and Class II
    rapids

Hazards: Swift currents, turbulence created by
    releases from the Lake Wylie Dam, shoals at
    Landsford Canal State Park

Runnable Water Level: Runnable year-round
    except during minimum releases

Suitable For: Beginners at low water,
    intermediates

Congaree River

The Congaree River, which delivers the bulk of the water in the Santee River watershed, makes a roundabout, 51.2-mile excursion from Columbia to the confluence with the Wateree River. The Congaree provides more than half the 12 billion gallons a day that flow into the upper Santee, which the Congaree forms with the Wateree. The Broad, Enoree, Pacolet, Reedy, and Saluda are among the major rivers that originate in both upstate South Carolina and western North Carolina and feed the Congaree.

In the early 1800s, the Congaree was part of a network of river routes that connected the Piedmont and central parts of South Carolina with the Lowcountry. Boats, barges, and steamships carrying cotton and other commodities sailed from Columbia to Charleston by way of the Congaree and the Santee. Steamships plied the Congaree as recently as the years just prior to World War I.

The 1934 act creating the S.C. Public Service Authority, known as Santee Cooper, envisioned commercial navigation up the Congaree to Columbia. The idea was dropped in the 1960s as being infeasible.

Before the creation of the Santee Cooper lakes in 1942, the Congaree fostered a large sturgeon fishery. Enterprising fishermen trapped Atlantic sturgeon for the caviar they yielded. Sturgeon weighing more than 300 pounds were documented. The dams impeded the sturgeon's migration up the Congaree.

Today, the river is still a fisherman's haven and, ironically, the same impoundment projects did not harm the striped bass fishery in the Congaree and Saluda Rivers. The migratory stripers were trapped behind the dams that formed Lakes Marion and Moultrie. Biologists at the time believed the fish would not be able to reproduce. But the stripers found the flowing waters of the Congaree and Saluda ideal as spawning grounds.

The Congaree borders South Carolina's largest national park, the 22,200-acre Congaree National Park.

As a canoeing river, most of the landings along the Congaree are too far apart for day trips. It's possible, but not feasible, for strong paddlers to cover the river from Columbia to U.S. 601 in one day. To float the Congaree, plan a two-day trip with an overnight stop on the river. While there is some high ground for camping, most of the land is private. Problems have arisen when disgruntled landowners discovered canoeists camping without permission.

Camping is allowed in the Congaree park. Campers can obtain a free permit by writing Congaree National Park, 100 National Park Road, Hopkins, SC 29061 or calling (803) 776-4396.

While it's possible to camp on sandbars, remember that releases from upstream dams on the Broad and Saluda can cause water to rise rapidly enough to cover a sandbar overnight.

The Congaree's current is usually brisk enough to make paddling fairly easy. The scenery is attractive, with few signs of civilization.

High bluffs border the river's right bank at intervals from the 20-mile mark to U.S. 601. Some have been excavated by archeologists searching for Indian artifacts. The highest bluff looms 323 feet. Just 5.0 miles upriver the elevation of the land is 110 feet.

U.S. 1-378 to Congaree Boat Ramp

The trail begins at the U.S. 1-378 bridge (A) in Columbia, which is Gervais Street.

The Senate Street public landing is on the east side of the bridge, about 100 yards downstream. The river contains submerged rocks for the first couple of miles, true to its Indian name that means "scraping place."

The Congaree Boat Ramp (B), dedicated in 1985, is 2.4 miles downstream on the left (east) side. This new landing is 1.3 miles east of S.C. 48 on S.C. 167 in Columbia.

Congaree Boat Ramp to Cayce Landing

The Cayce Landing (C) is 1.4 miles downstream on the right (west) side. Also known as the Congaree River Landing, it is off Old State Road, south of Cayce.

Cayce Landing to U.S. 601

It's 45.1 miles to the U.S. 601 bridge (D). The river's hazards consist of occasional snags, whirlpools, and fast-moving motorboats. Tricky currents in places make swimming dangerous.

There are few landmarks to measure mileage. A pronounced bend in the river called Devil's Elbow is 5.3 miles above the bridge.

At Devil's Elbow, the site of Fort Motte can be seen on a bluff on the right side. The home at the Motte plantation was established as a fort by the British in 1781. It was set on fire in an attack by patriot forces led by Francis Marion, the Swamp Fox, and Henry Lee. Although the house survived this attack, it burned a couple years later. This community was the home of Julia Peterkin, a Pulitzer Prize winner in 1928 for her novel *Scarlet Sister Mary*.

Railroad tracks cross the river 2.6 miles above the bridge. The U.S. 601 bridge public landing is on the left (east) side just below the bridge.

U.S. 601 to Tresvant Landing

From the bridge, the Wateree River is 1.9 miles away. The final take-out is Tresvant Landing (E), 1.4 miles below the confluence that forms the Santee.

From U.S. 601 at the Congaree, go south 2.0 miles and turn left (south) at S.C. 267, the Lone Star-Fort Motte crossroads. A sign marks the turnoff to the left a mile down S.C. 267.

Congaree River at a Glance

Trail: U.S.1-378 to Tresvant Landing on Santee River

Length: 52.6 miles

Topographic Maps: Elloree, Fort Jackson-South, Gadsden, Saylors Lake, Columbia-Southwest

County Maps: Calhoun, Lexington, Richland

Average Flow: 9,311 cubic feet or 250.7 million gallons per hour at U.S. 1-378 bridge in Columbia

Flood Stage: 19 feet at U.S. 1-378

Gradient: 30 feet or 0.6 feet per mile

Difficult: Flatwater

Hazards: Submerged rocks first two miles; snags, whirlpools, power boats, occasional instances of water rising overnight

Runnable Water Level: Runnable year-round

Suitable For: Beginners accompanied by intermediates

Congaree National Park

A float trip through the Congaree National Park along Cedar Creek can be a paddler's adventure and a naturalist's delight.

The park, 20 miles southeast of Columbia, contains the last significant tract of old-growth bottomland hardwoods in the southeastern United States. This floodplain (not a true swamp) became a national monument, a unit of the National Park Service, in 1976 after a concerted citizens' effort to save its uncut stands of giant trees from logging. It was designated a park in 2003.

The 22,200-acre preserve has over 80 species of trees, among them 29 individual trees that are of record size, either state or national champions. The thickest tree is a bald cypress that measures 26 feet in circumference. A loblolly pine that stands 167 fee high and is nearly 15 feet around holds the state size record. Several trees are more than 160 feet tall, making the canopy among the highest in a temperate-zone deciduous forest anywhere.

Wildlife in the grove-like forest is abundant. The park teems with birds, mammals, reptiles, and fish. Otters, turkey, bobcat, deer, feral hogs, raccoon, and opossum are common. The last wild hog taken by hunters from the swamp weighed 500 pounds. The swamp is within the range of a band of black bears from the Wateree River floodplain. Snakes are abundant but the nonpoisonous brown water snake by far outnumbers the poisonous water moccasin. Barred owls, pileated woodpeckers, and red-tailed hawks are among the larger birds.

Floating the Congaree park means paddling Cedar Creek, which meanders through the swamp, crisscrossing other creeks and branches, locally called "guts," for 14.8 miles before flowing into the Congaree River. The more ambitious paddler might try an overnight trip through the swamp and take out at the U.S. 601 bridge on the Congaree River. It's about 20 miles—actual mileage is difficult to compute because of all the twists and turns in the creek.

The park is a federally designated wilderness area. The canoe trail is primitive with extreme variances in water levels due to flooding. There are numerous downed trees that require portages. It would be in the paddler's best interest to contact the park before leaving on a canoe trip to check for current conditions. The swamp is periodically inundated with water from heavy Upstate runoffs. When this happens, the floodwaters sometimes create false channels, channels that don't show up on topographic maps. The danger of taking a wrong turn and getting lost is real.

A number of streams flow into the river and Cedar Creek flows in at two different points. During flooding of the Congaree River, resulting reverse flows in the feeder streams can be confusing. Getting lost may mean an extra overnight stay, so pack extra food and water. As long as you follow the flow, you should eventually end up in the river, though perhaps not where you had planned. Float groups should stay together and not split up in an effort to find a way out.

Camping is allowed anywhere in the park with some restrictions, but it requires a free camping permit that can be obtained at the visitor center. Write the park at Congaree National Park, 100 National Park Road, Hopkins, SC 29061 or call (803) 776-4396.

The entrance to the park is on a paved road off S-734 (Old Bluff Road). From I-77 travel 12 miles southeast to S.C. 48. Turn right onto Old Bluff Road and follow the signs to the visitor center.

S-734 to Cedar Creek Road

The first put-in on Cedar Creek is at Bannister's Bridge on S-734 (A).

Directions on where to leave vehicles can be obtained at the visitor center, which is open from 8:30 a.m. to 5:00 p.m. every day except Christmas. The park is open daily from dawn until dusk.

The first section of Cedar Creek winds through brush and forest. Some of the magnificent loblolly pines are visible about a mile down on the left. This 5.2-mile segment also affords some views of large oaks and tupelos. It takes two to three hours to reach Wise Lake, the first metal bridge. Nearby is a clearing that used to be the site of an old hunting lodge. Shortly after putting in again, the floater will come to a fork in the creek. Take the channel to the left.

The Cedar Creek Road Parking Area (B) is another two hours downstream.

Cedar Creek Road to U.S. 601

To reach Cedar Creek Road (S-1288), continue east on S-734 until it dead-ends, into Cedar Creek Road, then turn right (south). A gravel road closed off by a pipe gate leads to the throw-in access. This is an alternative starting point that can knock off several hours from the trip to the U.S. 601 bridge.

About 2.0 miles downstream from the second roadbed the creek splits again. While the right fork appears to be the larger, it's a dead end. Take the left fork. About 0.5 mile farther a hand-dug canal, perhaps dating to the early nineteenth century, is a shortcut. Back on the main channel, some high ground offers good campsites.

The first real navigation puzzle in this 16.3-mile section crops up just beyond a lake. Here, the channel splits again. Bear to the left even though it is narrow with downfalls. At low water the going will be tough. The channel is difficult to find during high water, and low-hanging limbs extend over the creek.

The next decision comes about a mile later where the creek twists hard to the left. Another stream, Horsepen, bears straight ahead and leads to the Congaree River, about 4.0 miles upstream from the spot where Cedar Creek enters. This is also a major source of inflow during flooding. In fact, at high water it might seem that you are paddling upstream as much as 2.0 miles on Cedar Creek because of the reverse flow created by flooding. To stay on Cedar Creek, bear left at the juncture of the two streams and the flow will be downstream again.

About 3.0 miles away two streams come in from the river right and another from the left. The streams to the right, called Mazyk Cutoff, branch off into several mouths that lead to the Congaree River. Take the streams to the right, through Mazyk's Cutoff and you will arrive shortly at the Congaree River. Take a left turn at the Congaree River and float 11.0 miles to the U.S. 601 bridge (C) and a paved public landing on the left (north) side of the bridge.

⌐_⟋_⌐ Congaree Park at a Glance
       Trail: Cedar Creek at S-734 to U.S. 601 on
           Congaree River
       Length: 21.5 miles
       Topographic Map: Gadsden, Wateree
       County Map: Richland
       Average Flow: Not available
       Flood Stage: Not established
       Gradient: 19 feet or 0.9 feet per mile
       Hazards: Channels hard to follow in high water;
           downfalls, snags, strainers, possibility of get-
           ting lost
       Difficulty: Flatwater
       Runnable Water Level: May be too difficult in late
           summer and fall when water is low
       Suitable For: Beginners on guided tours; interme-
           diates with at least one advanced member in
           the party

Enoree River

The Cherokee Indians gave the river the name Enoree, which means "river of muscadines." The name still fits this Piedmont river, as a trip down most any part of the lower sections will confirm. Trees along the banks of the meandering Enoree are draped with the dark-green muscadine grape vine, creating the appearance of an unruly vineyard.

The Enoree (pronounced EN-or-ee) wends its way through the lower Piedmont and Sumter National Forest before giving up its identity to the Broad River. It's an ideal river for experienced flatwater paddlers who like the push of a peppy current and the split-second zig-zags required to maneuver around fallen trees.

Foliage along much of the lower Enoree is particularly lush, a mixture of water oak, ash, sycamore, and hickory trees, plus poison ivy and, of course, grape vine. The trees arch over the reddish-brown water, forming a natural cathedral.

The surrounding pine and hardwood forests harbor deer, turkey, and red-shouldered hawks. The river supports great blue herons, barred owls, wood ducks, osprey, mink, muskrat, and otter.

An antebellum house, Cross Keys, stands north of the Enoree in Union County at the intersection of S.C. 49 and S-22, 10 miles southwest of Union. Built 1812–14 by Barrum Bobo, the house was the center of a prosperous plantation. It also figured momentarily in the final days of the Confederacy. On April 30, 1865, President Jefferson Davis lunched at the house during his flight from Richmond, Virginia, to Georgia.

S.C. 49 to S.C. 56

The 61.2-mile trail begins at the S.C. 49 bridge (A) at the Laurens and Spartanburg County line. Park on the east (Spartanburg) side of the bridge and use either side of the river as a launch point for this 6.5-mile section.

In the first few hundred yards, the Enoree has a series of channels and rapids ranging from Class I to Class III in high water. Stick to the right channel to catch the drops or, if you prefer, seek out the other channels to the left for a less challenging ride. Caution: These rapids can become dangerous in high water because of the sharp drops and numerous boulders.

Beyond this point the Enoree has only a few riffles and Class I water for the next 10 miles or so. The first access after S.C. 49 is the S.C. 56 bridge (B), a throw-in. Take out on either side.

S.C. 56 to S-22-98

The S-22-98 bridge (C) is 5.5 miles and two hours downstream. Take out on the right just below the bridge, Jones Bridge.

S-22-98 to U.S. 176-S.C. 72-121

The Sumter National Forest begins here. For the next 16.4 miles, the Enoree pushes along lazily. A mile downstream, floaters will pass under a 100-foot bridge that's part of the Palmetto Trail, the Enoree Passage. About 10 miles downstream, bluffs and high ridges appear.

A Forest Service boat ramp (D) is on the north (left) side a half mile above U.S. 176-S.C. 72-121. From Whitmire in Newberry County, follow U.S. 176-S.C. 72-121 north to S-18; go west on S-18 to Lee Cemetery Road; turn left (south) on Forest Service Road 339 and follow it to the landing.

U.S. 176-S.C. 72-121 to S-81

While the lower Enoree is languid in summer, it's a delight in winter and spring when rains reinvigorate the current.

The next access is 9.7 miles away at the S-81 bridge, Brazzleman's Bridge (E). Access is on the left (east) side and the ramp has been paved. Here, the Enoree speeds up in places where it is constricted, forcing paddlers to run a gauntlet of limbs and trees. Keep an eye out for wasp nests on low branches.

S-81 to S-45

The last access before the confluence with the Broad is 5.5 miles away at the S-45 bridge, Keitt's Bridge (F). Take out on the right (south) side just below the bridge.

S-45 to S.C. 34

From Keitt's Bridge, it's just 4.0 miles and less than two hours to the Broad and another hour to S.C. 34 (G). There's no access at the bridge. Take out 50 yards below the bridge on the left (east) side at a primitive landing.

From the highway, turn off at the first road east of the S.C. 34 bridge.

Enoree River at a Glance

Trail: S.C. 49 to S.C. 34 on Broad River

Length: 61.2 miles

Topographic Maps: Blair, Ora, Philson Crossroads, Pomaris, Sedalia, Whitmire-North, Whitmire-South

County Maps: Fairfield, Laurens, Newberry, Spartanburg, Union

Average Flow: 600 cubic feet per second or 16.2 million gallons per hour at U.S. 176-S.C. 72-121

Flood Stage: Not established

Gradient: 160 feet or 3.4 feet per mile

Difficulty: Class I–III in upper section; fast flatwater, flatwater in lower sections

Hazards: Steep drops in upper section; deadfalls, strainers, wasp nests in lower sections

Runnable Water Level: Runnable year-round; upper section may be dangerous in high water

Suitable For: Intermediate in upper section; beginners in lower sections

photo by Jack Horan

Paddlers can launch at Givhans Ferry State Park on the Edisto River.

Saluda River, Upper Section

Cascading out of mountains in Greenville and Pickens Counties, the Saluda River is fragmented by dams and lakes on its course through the western Piedmont. Two sections of the Saluda, however, have extensive free-flowing parts and the section near Columbia has the only whitewater in the Midlands.

The first section, between Lake Greenwood and Lake Murray, spans 32.8 miles through hardwood forests. The second, a 9.5-mile segment from Lake Murray to the Broad River, lends an air of wilderness to an urban setting in the Columbia area.

The Saluda, from a site near Ninety Six in Greenwood County called Buzzard's Roost to Columbia, parallels the old Cherokee Path, an Indian trail of colonial times that opened the way to the foothills of the Blue Ridge Mountains.

In 1715, a member of an expedition to enlist the aid of the Cherokees on behalf of white settlers in their fight against the coastal Yemassee Indians wrote, "We killed a boflow on this day." He was referring to the buffalo, or American bison, that roamed the Piedmont before hunters and settlers killed off the animal.

Later, the Cherokee Path would become the first backwoods road connecting the Upcountry to Charleston. In 1737, a trading post was established at a place marked on an early map as "96," the present site of the town of Ninety Six.

The lake-to-lake float beginning at Lake Greenwood dam on S.C. 34 is a delightful section teeming with wildlife. Clear water makes it easy to spot golden-tinted carp, silvery striped bass, an occasional catfish or largemouth bass, and many bream.

On one autumn trip, paddlers counted three species of turtles, seven otters, a slain deer being hauled up a bank by hunters, great blue herons, kingfishers, wood ducks, and a gallinule. Black buzzards and turkey vultures share roosts in trees about 1.0 mile downriver from the first put-in. A fisherman tending trot lines below Kempson's Bridge hauled in a carp he judged to be a 10-pounder.

Under normal water conditions, the entire trip takes about ten and a half hours. Add two hours to that total on summer weekends and in the fall when the water level is down. Although a railroad closely follows the river for about 12.0 miles, it seldom comes into view through the trees, which provides a sense of isolation.

S.C. 34 to S.C. 121

Put in at the S.C. 34 bridge (A) on the right (west) side above the bridge. An alternate put-in 9.3 miles downstream is the S.C. 39 bridge from a rough access road on river right (west). It is a throw-in with a steep bank.

The 20.8-mile float to Higgins Bridge at S.C. 121 (B) has numerous rock ledges and sandy banks with an assortment of hardwoods bordering the river. When the water is down, which it is every weekend when the dam at Lake Greenwood is closed, the reduced flow creates mild Class II rapids over two of the rock ledges. A few riffles and Class I rapids crop up here and there.

For the most part, the rapids are straightforward. Just pick out the "V" and follow the line through the standing waves. One rapid, however, requires a hard right draw to avoid lodging in some rocks.

Take out at the Heller public landing about 100 feet below S.C. 121 on the left (north) side. An alternative take-out two miles farther downstream on the left is the Saluda River Resort, a commercial boat landing and camping area.

S.C. 121 to S.C. 395

The next landfall is Kempson's Bridge at S.C. 395 (C), 6.7 miles downstream. From this point, the river widens and the current slows significantly. Lake Murray begins here, forming wide, sweeping bends, coves, and backwater arms. Fishermen and boat traffic become more frequent.

At S.C. 395, take out on the left (east) side below the bridge.

S.C. 395 to S.C. 391

The last take-out on this 5.4-mile section is Morris public landing on the left (north) side just above the S.C. 391 bridge, Black's Bridge, (D). Another public landing is on the right side of the river.

Saluda River, Upper Section, at a Glance
Trail: S.C. 34 to S.C. 391
Length: 32.8 miles
Topographic Maps: Chappells, Delmar, Dyson, Silverstreet
County Maps: Greenwood, Newberry, Saluda
Average Flow: 1,967 cubic feet per second or 53.0 million gallons per hour at S.C. 39 bridge
Flood Stage: 14 feet at S.C. 39 (Chappells)
Gradient: 30 feet, or 0.9 feet per mile
Difficulty: Fast flatwater—Class I-II at lower water, flat water last 7.0 miles
Hazards: Some rock ledges in first 5.0 miles; strainers when water is high
Runnable Water Level: Upper part may be difficult

when water is low on weekends during late
summer
Suitable For: Beginners accompanied by
intermediates

Saluda River, Lower Section

The Saluda from the Lake Murray Dam to the confluence with the Broad at Columbia contains nearly 3.0 miles of dam-release whitewater, making the stretch a lively and popular run for canoeists and kayakers.

The rapids are as strong—and as dangerous—under heavy flow conditions as some of those on the Chattooga River. One rapid, Mill Race, attains a Class V or possibly Class VI rating when the dam is discharging the maximum 18,000 cubic feet of water per second.

The river is rife with rock mazes that cause the water to behave differently at various levels. While the river usually can be floated without incident on weekends, unscheduled water releases from the dam can turn the Saluda into a raging torrent in a matter of minutes.

Canoeists and kayakers who regularly paddle the 9.5-mile section contend that, because water levels can fluctuate from 400 to 18,000 cubic feet, the river is like 10 different rivers. The average flow is 2,896 cubic feet.

Some rapids are more likely to be created by low or moderate water levels. Where there are impassable rock mazes at lower water, high flow turns them into Class III-IV whitewater.

The upshot of all this is that the lower Saluda can be a pussycat or a lion. The river is for capable paddlers who are familiar with the various levels. Otherwise, a trip could invite disaster.

In 1983, for example, 16 paddlers embarked on what they thought would be a laid-back float trip. Their first mistake was entering the river at flood stage. Before they could reach the spot where they planned to take out and portage Mill Race, operators at the Lake Murray Dam opened all five turbines. In a matter of minutes, the river became so turbulent the current swept several canoes into Mill Race. Three canoes were wrecked, a couple of paddlers were trapped for a time in a strong hydraulic, another was marooned and several sustained minor injuries.

On that same day, a paddler who had run the river many times went through Mill Race and came out with a separated shoulder.

Paddlers can obtain information on releases from the Lake Murray Dam by calling South Carolina Electric & Gas Co.'s Lake Murray Hotline at (800) 830-5253 or

(803) 217-8399 anytime.

The Saluda, from a mile below the dam to the confluence with the Broad River, has been designated a state Scenic River. The designation grew out of a campaign by Save Our Saluda Inc. after the utility proposed a feasibility study for a dam on the river that would have eliminated the rapids. The utility withdrew its application for the study in 1983, and in 1985 agreed to donate a 100-foot easement along 37 percent of the riverbank.

The temperature of the water near the dam is cold enough (50-60 degrees Fahrenheit) to support stocked trout. Largemouth bass, striped bass, and white bass live in the river.

Historically, the river played a major part in the growth of Columbia. The Saluda Canal, which operated from about 1820 to 1837, helped to make the Saluda navigable for 120 miles above Columbia. The remains of the 2.5-mile-long canal, which had five locks, can be seen on the left bank below the Riverbanks Zoo.

Lake Murray Dam to U.S. 1-378
The first two access points below the dam face each other across the river. On the north side is the Saluda Shoals Regional Park (A), off Bush River Road, while the Hope Ferry Landing (now, James R. Metts Landing) is off Corley Mill Road.

Another put-in is Gardendale (B), off Bush River Road, 3.5 miles downriver.

The first 6.5 miles to I-26 are flatwater except for a few riffles. The first rapids are 200 yards below the bridge, after the river divides. The right channel goes to Oh Brother Rapids; the left route goes to Ocean Boulevard. Oh Brother Rapids, to the right of a small island submerged at high water, has about 20 yards of rapids that run from Class II in low water to Class III in high water. Run them straight on.

Alternatively, on the left side, is Ocean Boulevard, a rock maze at low water and a Class IV at high water. The river creates souse holes at Ocean Boulevard when the level is just under high water. Stick to the right.

Stacy's Ledge crops up 0.5 mile downstream. The lower edge is marked by a red pier on the left bank. The ledge is about 25 feet wide. Below it is a strong hydraulic. To avoid the hydraulic, run the rapid to the left of the ledge about 25 feet from the bank or to the far right side of the river. About 50 yards below the ledge, just right of center, is a hole where kayakers can surf when the water is up.

The rapid to the left of Stacy's Ledge rates a high Class III to Class IV while the right-side run is Class IV. Both become a Class II at low water.

The red pier is an important landmark for those who want to portage dangerous Mill Race Rapids and that should include everyone. The portage landfall on the right bank is a well-marked spot below Stacy's Ledge around a bend in the river. It's a short portage around Mill Race to a sandy beach.

It's also possible to portage on the left side, although the distance is several hundred yards. This might be the wiser choice when the water is rising since a quick current that moves right to left can make it difficult to land on the right bank.

Mill Race, which is about 250 yards past Stacy's Ledge, is the site of an old coffer dam that was blasted away. The remnants include sharp, jagged rocks and protruding metal rods. Even experienced whitewater paddlers can misread the water in Mill Race, which has several keeper holes. At low water, Mill Race is virtually impassable. At high water, the safest route for skilled whitewater boaters is on the left side of Mill Race

Shandon Rapids is about 0.75 mile below the re-entry after portaging Millrace. The rapids are rated Class IV in high water, which creates keeper hydraulics on the left side and standing waves from 4 to 5 feet. The recommended course is to the right at high water.

Riverbanks Zoo is on the left bank between Millrace and Shandon Rapids.

White House Rapids is 200 yards downstream from Shandon Rapids near Broad River. The river is very wide at this point, permitting a number of routes through this Class II at high water.

The Hampton Street Bridge Rapids begin just above the bridge in the Congaree River, formed by the Saluda and the Broad. Several chutes provide passage at low water, but high levels increase the rapids to Class IV with 5-foot standing waves. These waves reach 8 feet when both rivers are running high.

The take-out is on the left (east) side below U.S. 1-378 (Gervais Street) bridge (C). This is the Senate Street public landing.

Saluda River, Lower Section, at a Glance

Trail: Lake Murray Dam to U.S. 1-378

Length: 9.5 miles

Topographic Maps: Columbia-North, Irmo, Columbia-Southwest

County Maps: Lexington, Richland

Average Flow: 2,896 cubic feet per second or 78.0 million gallons per hour at Old Saluda Mill site, 1.6 miles above Broad River confluence

Flood Stage: Not established

Gradient: 45 feet or 4.7 feet per mile

Difficulty: Class IV-V in high water to fast flatwater

Hazards: Rock mazes, rock ledges, submerged
rocks, strong hydraulics, sharp rocks, and
protruding metal rods at Mill Race Rapids.
Rapidly rising water than can change the
rating of rapids in minutes.
Runnable Water Level: Runnable year-round
except at flood stage
Suitable For: Intermediates and advanced
depending on water levels, beginners only
when accompanied by advanced paddlers
who know the river

Turkey-Stevens Creeks

Stevens Creek begins in the heart of McCormick County, eventually joining Turkey Creek to form part of the boundary between McCormick and Edgefield Counties. These creeks course through relatively undeveloped woodlands and flow into the Savannah River just above North Augusta.

The headwaters of Stevens Creek form near the village of Plum Branch, just a few miles from McCormick, once a nineteenth-century boom town named Dorn's Gold Mine. The creeks and branches that feed Stevens Creek and Turkey Creek were panned for gold and led prospectors to richer deposits in rock formations.

The Sumter National Forest borders much of both creeks. To protect the natural experience along the creeks, the U.S. Forest Service established a 1,070-acre corridor that bars timber cutting within 100 feet of the banks. The corridor includes the national forest lands that comprise about two-thirds of the shoreline between S.C. 283 on Turkey Creek to the confluence with Stevens Creek, and along Stevens Creek to within 1.0 mile of S-88.

The protection includes the state-designated Stevens Creek Natural Area, a geological and botanical oddity. Rock outcroppings more commonly found in the mountains and several rare mountain flowers are found in and around Stevens Creek. The natural area is a wildflower paradise and supports a hardwood forest thought to be a relic from a glacial period.

One of the most striking wildflowers found along the banks is the stately and vivid red lobelia of summer and early fall. Among the botanical oddities of Stevens Creek is the presence of large bald cypresses and cypress knees. The cypress grow close to the water's edge at the base of the bluffs and form an intriguing mix with large sycamores, American ash, elms, oaks, and cottonwoods.

Wildlife along the creeks is varied. Stealthy paddlers can see deer and turkey. In summer, when the water level is normal or low, catfish, bass, bream, and garfish, as well as clams and mussels, are easily visible in the clear water. Birdlife is abundant and includes kingfishers, pileated woodpeckers, red-tailed hawks, little blue herons, and great blue herons.

Float times on the creeks vary with water levels. In the high-water months of spring and early summer, the run from S.C. 283 to S.C. 23 can be made in five to six hours. In late summer or early fall, when water levels are down, the trip could take eight hours or longer. High water should preclude float plans on these creeks because of strainers, logjams, and the difficulty of portaging the steep banks. The creeks should be considered dangerous to run in early spring, and paddlers should be aware of flash flood threats from heavy rain.

The Forest Service cleaned out the 12-mile section that runs through the Sumter National Forest in 1984.

Paddlers can camp on national forest land. Contact the District Ranger, 810 Buncombe Street, Edgefield, S.C. 29824, (803) 637-5396, for a free permit. Campers should be aware that posted, privately owned property is mixed with public land.

S.C. 283 to S-227

The first recommended put-in on Turkey Creek is at the S.C. 283 bridge (A) 3.7 miles west of Brunson Crossroads and 10 miles west of Edgefield. A set of steps leads from a parking area on the left (east) side of the creek.

From here, it's a 4.0-mile float to the S-227 bridge, Key Bridge, (B).

At Key Bridge, a primitive dirt road leads south from the paved road down the east bank. Park at the edge of the wildlife opening and carry canoes down a set of steps to the stream about 100 yards downstream from the abandoned steel bridge.

S-227 to S.C. 23

The two creeks meet 3.5 miles downstream to form a larger Stevens Creek.

The next take-out is the S.C. 23 bridge, Modoc Bridge, (C) 4.5 miles below the confluence.

There is an access on the right (east) side below the bridge as well as one on the left (west) side upstream from the bridge. The west side access has a short set of stairs down the bank. A 200-yard-long trail leads to a parking lot. The bridge is 1.4 miles east of U.S. 221-S.C. 28.

S.C. 23 to Stevens Creek Park

Below S.C. 23 in this 10.0-mile section, a take-out is possible at the Stevens

Creek Natural Area. The take-out, however, is difficult to spot and requires scouting. Above the Natural Area, the creek runs in a virtual straight line, then bends sharply to the east. The Natural Area is situated on the right (west) bank. You will know you've missed your landfall if you reach the S-88-143 bridge, 0.25 mile downstream.

The unusual course of Stevens Creek, which takes a right-angle turn above Modoc Bridge and an almost 90-degree turn below the Natural Area, may be due to the influence of a geological fault.

From the S-88-143 bridge, Cary Hill Bridge, it's 6.0 miles to the landing on S-53 (Woodlawn Road) on the right (east) side. The turnoff to the boat ramp is 3.5 miles below the junction of S.C. 230 and S-143 about 0.25 mile to the right.

The trail ends at the Stevens Creek Park (D) 3.0 miles downstream. The last 7.0 miles are radically different from the upper part of the creek. The high bluffs that predominate upstream give way to flat terrain. The Stevens Creek Dam on the Savannah River backs up the water, slows the current and creates lake-like conditions to make paddling slow and arduous.

Take out at the park on the left (south) side.

To reach the park, turn left (west) at the intersection of S-402 at S.C. 230 2.3 miles north of the Aiken-Edgefield county line. Follow S-402, then bear right on S-432 and right again on S-433. The park is at the end of a gravel road.

Turkey-Stevens Creeks At a Glance
Trail: S.C. 283 to Stevens Creek Park
Length: 22.0 miles
Topographic Maps: Clarks Hill, Colliers, Limestone, Parksville, Red Hill
County Maps: Edgefield, McCormick
Average Flow: Not available
Flood Stage: Not established
Gradient: 50 feet or 2.3 feet per mile
Difficulty: Fast flatwater in upper sections; flatwater in lower sections
Hazards: Deadfalls, submerged logs, occasional rocks, steep banks. Creeks can rise 15 to 20 feet in a few hours after hard rain.
Runnable Water Level: Upper sections should not be attempted at low-water levels in late summer and fall.
Suitable For: Beginners

Tyger River

This lively, occasionally frolicking stream spills across the Piedmont south of Spartanburg before sliding through the Sumter National Forest, where it joins the Broad River. The rocky upper reaches of the Tyger offer about 15 miles of Class I and Class II rapids, a delight for paddlers looking for some nearby whitewater and for novices who want to practice their river skills. Be aware that heavy rains can increase the difficulty of the rapids.

The lower three-fourths of the Tyger has no whitewater, save for a riffle here and there. But its usually brisk flatwater gives a nice ridge to paddlers who want to explore the Sumter forest and its mixture of pines and hardwoods, slopes, and bluffs. Lining the banks of the river, and often leaning over to form a graceful arch, are sweet gum, water oak, sycamore, cottonwood, and river birch trees.

Turkey have become plentiful in the Sumter forest and the chance of seeing one fly over the river is good. Other creatures that can be seen are deer, great blue herons, and southern banded water snakes.

Be aware, though, that the Tyger can act like a tiger when spring rains come. Swift water coupled with logs and strainers can turn the pleasant stream into a tricky and dangerous river. Choose campsites carefully; the river can rise rapidly.

The Tyger is believed to have derived its name either from a French fur trader named Tygert or a legend that says a tiger (probably a panther) and a bear fought on the banks of the river. The tiger, of course, emerged the winner.

The river area was the scene of an important Revolutionary War battle more than 200 years ago. At Blackstock's Plantation, just inside Union County near the Spartanburg County line, Col. Thomas Sumter's American soldiers fought British colonel Banastre Tarleton and his troops to a standstill on November 20, 1780.

The upper part of the Tyger consists of two tributaries, the North Tyger and the South Tyger. The North Tyger section will be listed first in the trail description, followed by the South Tyger. The two streams merge just above the S-50 bridge.

A proposed lake threatens the lower Tyger; a dam at the Fairforest Creek confluence would create a 5,300-acre reservoir.

S-231 to S-113

The North Tyger trail begins in the rolling woodlands of Spartanburg County at the S-231 bridge (A). From the bridge, Marches Bridge, the river drops 56 feet in the 4.0-mile run to S-50.

After some high bluffs and rock outcroppings, Nancy Thomas Shoals appears.

Run this Class I-II by going down the right side or straight down the center. Harrison Shoals, which is next, is more like a 50-yard-long washboard. Run this Class II straight ahead.

After Harrison Shoals is Nesbitt Shoals, a Class II that is a quarter-mile jaunt through a maze of rocks and ledges. An intermediate take-out is at the S-50 bridge on the right (south) side just above the bridge.

Below the bridge, another set of shoals are around the first bend in this 3.2-mile segment. Keep to the right because of protruding rods in the middle and on the left.

The best rapid on this section may be the Class II one-third of a mile above the S-113 bridge (B). It is a series of ledges. In the middle, on the right, is a surfing wave below a drop.

Take out at the S-113 bridge on the right (south) side just below the bridge.

S-86 to S-50

An alternative put-in is the South Tyger. This 4.4-mile section meets the North Tyger just above Nesbitt Shoals and, combined with the preceding section, can make a day of paddling.

photo by Jack Horan

Tyger River offers an easy glide through the Upstate.

To reach the put-in at Ferguson's Creek on S-86 (C).

Run the first large rapid, Susan Thomas Shoals, from right to left. At the next rapid, Chesnee Shoals, start at the left and then bear to the right. Both are Class IIs.

Take out at S-50 (D).

S-113 to S.C. 49

At the S-113 bridge (B), the rocky shoals split the Tyger into several channels that make 2-foot-high drops. Follow the right channels if you want to avoid the 7-foot-high, two-step rapid, a Class III and possible Class IV in high water. The channels on each side spread through islands and trees and, in low water, a portage may be necessary.

After the first quarter mile, the Tyger loses its punch and becomes a flatwater river in the 13.4-mile stretch to the S.C. 49 bridge (E).

A rough take-out is possible at the S.C. 56 bridge, 6.2 miles below S-113.

S.C. 49 to U.S. 176

The access at the S.C. 49 bridge, Cedar Bluff Bridge, requires a 50-yard walk down the left (north) bank. This is the boundary of the Sumter National Forest and the beginning of a 13.8-mile section.

The river, now about 30 yards wide, is mostly clear of debris to the next landmark, the remains of Minter's Bridge, about two hours downstream.

Seven miles downriver is S-16 bridge, Gist Bridge, just after the Rose Hill public landing on the right (south) side. Rose Hill State Park, just south of the river on S-16, was named after the 1828 mansion of William Henry Gist, secessionist governor of South Carolina from 1858 to 1860. The mansion is noted for its fanlights, carved doors, and spiral staircases.

Beyond Gist Bridge, the Tyger becomes a minor obstacle course, cluttered with logs, stumps, and trees that have toppled into the water. Small bluffs, covered with ferns, are set against the forest of cedars and sycamores.

At the U.S. 176 bridge (F), take out on the left (north) side of the river at the paved Beatty's Bridge landing.

U.S. 176 to S.C. 35-54

The river widens to about 125 feet, making leisurely turns on its way to the S.C. 72-121 bridge 5.8 miles away. Access at the bridge is difficult. Be sure to pause to watch the blue-and-orange barn swallows that live under the bridge swoop up and down the river.

Along this next 12.5-mile section, the Tyger constricts and resembles an overgrown brook, gurgling pleasantly as it flows over debris.

Five miles downstream is one of the prettiest spots on the Tyger. As the river makes a bend to the left, a 30-foot-high bluff looms over the south bank. Mountain laurel clings to the bluff's craggy face. Limestone rocks jut into the river, forcing the current into a deep pool rimmed by a sandy beach.

At the S.C. 35-54 bridge, Gardon's Bridge, (G) take out on the right (south) side just before the bridge.

S-35-54 to S.C. 34

The Tyger drifts 3.7 miles to its confluence with the Broad, which in turn passes through a riffly section around Henderson Island.

At the S.C. 34 bridge (H), take out on the left (east) bank at a primitive landing. To get to the landing from S. C. 34, take the first road east of the bridge.

Tyger River at a Glance

Trail: S-231 and S-86 to S.C. 34 on Broad River

Length: 62.6 miles

Topographic Maps: Blair, Cross Anchor, Moore, Sedalia, Union-West, Whitmire-North, Whitmire-South

County Maps: Fairfield, Newberry, Spartanburg, Union

Average Flow: 1,142 cubic feet per second or 30.8 million gallons per hour at S.C. 72-121

Flood Stage: Not established

Gradient: 297 feet or 4.7 feet per mile

Difficulty: Class I-III on the upper sections, fast flatwater

Hazards: Steep ledges and extensive shoals in upper sections, logs and strainers in lower sections

Runnable Water Level: Runnable year-round although low flow in late summer and fall may make some shoals hard to get through

Suitable For: Intermediates in upper sections, beginners accompanied by intermediates in lower sections

Wateree River

From the Lake Wateree Dam to the river's confluence with the Congaree River to form the Santee, the Wateree makes a 77.6-mile trek across the Fall Line and through floodplain terrain. It's a river that offers topography varying from swampland to a chain of ridges called the Hills of Santee.

The Wateree, which is the Catawba River above Lake Wateree, begins in Kershaw County, forms the boundary between Richland and Sumter Counties, and ends in Calhoun County. The name is taken from a Siouan Indian tribe that inhabited the valley until about 1715.

The Wateree flows through an area rich with history and tradition.

George Washington crossed the river during his travels as a young man, and Revolutionary War general Thomas Sumter is buried in the woodlands of the Wateree floodplain where he led his partisan forces in skirmishes against the British.

The Revolutionary War Park of Camden is just to the east of the Wateree in an area known for steeplechases, polo, and fox hunting. Much of the land adjacent to the river is managed by hunting clubs. Deer are plentiful and during fall they often swim the river to elude hunters and dogs.

Turkey inhabit the bluffs and woods beside the river. Wood ducks, great blue herons, hawks, osprey, kingfishers, anhingas, pileated woodpeckers, and many species of smaller birds are commonly seen.

At one time steamers from the Lowcountry came upriver to Camden with the help of a U.S. Army Corps of Engineers project that deepened the channel. The project was abandoned in 1915 because of the high cost of maintenance.

The Wateree is famous for its huge catfish. Many caught in the lower section weigh upward of fifty pounds. Striped bass from the Santee Cooper lakes also migrate up the Wateree.

Marked changes take place in the floodplain as the river moves across the Fall Line. Spanish moss begins to drape many trees about 30 miles below the dam. The trees range from sycamore, maple, and large oak to willow, cypress, cottonwood, and poplar.

The river, because of the drop in elevation and the large number of feeder creeks, maintains a lively current that makes paddling easy even when the water is low.

Scheduled releases are planned at the Wateree Dam. See page 151.

Lake Wateree Dam to U.S. 1-601

The first access is just below the Lake Wateree Dam (A) at the Lugoff public landing off S-37. The ramp is at the end of a gravel road to the right just past the

"End of State Maintenance" sign.

The Wateree runs in pretty much a straight line for the first 7.4 miles, passing farmland and other signs of civilization.

The take-out at U.S. 1-601 bridge (B) is below the bridge on the right (west) side.

U.S. 1-601 to U.S. 76-378

From here, the next take-out is 43.3 miles away. During late winter and spring when the river is running high, it's possible for strong paddlers to make the distance in a long day's run.

It's better, however, to make an overnight trip and do this section in two days. When water is high, good camping areas are scarce from about 20 miles above the landing at the U.S. 76-378 bridge (C). A good landmark about 27 miles downriver is a gravel bank on the right (west) bank belonging to a hunting club.

From that point on, camping sites are hard to find. It's no problem to find camp-sites at low and moderate water levels.

The Wateree doesn't begin to lose the sounds of traffic from nearby highways until it starts making sweeping turns through Betty Neck Swamp below I-20. The first of the great bluffs appears near Raglin Creek. Then swamp forests take over again on both sides of the river—broad floodplains filled with branches and lakes.

Seven miles beyond the U.S. 76-378 landing, Cook's Mountain rises abruptly on the right side as the river makes a southwestern turn. Although its 372-foot summit is modest, this ironstone-capped remnant of the Hills of Santee is impressive, rising as it does from a tupelo-cypress swamp. It has a unique ecology in which beech and mountain laurel grow within a few feet of swamp ash and water oak.

These conditions are repeated when the river passes about 0.5 mile west of Poinsett State Park on its last leg below U.S. 76-378.

The public landing at U.S. 76-378, called the Highway 76 landing, is on the right (west) bank between the bridges. This is where Garners Ferry provided passage across the river for travelers between Columbia and Sumter until a bridge was built in 1922.

U.S. 76-378 to Tresvant Landing

This 26.9-mile section ends at Tresvant Landing (D), a public access marked as Saw Dust Landing on the Calhoun County road map.

Two railroad tracks that cross the river serve as landmarks. The first is 10.7 miles below U.S. 76-378; the second is 5.2 miles farther, or 15.9 miles downriver. Near the end of the Wateree is International Paper's Eastover paper mill, formerly

Union Camp, which opened in 1984.

Tresvant Landing is 1.4 miles below the confluence with the Congaree, which enters from the right. This marks the beginning of the Santee River.

From U.S. 601 at the Congaree River, go south 2.0 miles and turn left (east) at S.C. 267, the Lone Star-Fort Motte crossroads. A sign marks the turnoff to the left a mile down S.C. 267. After Tresvant Landing, the Santee soon flows into the backwater of Lake Marion and Sparkleberry Swamp.

Wateree River at a Glance

Trail: Lake Wateree Dam to Tresvant Landing on
    Santee River

Length: 77.6 miles

Topographic Maps: Camden, Camden-South,
    Eastover, Elloree, Leesburg, Lugoff, Poinsett
    State Park, Rembert, Wateree, Wedgefield

County Maps: Calhoun, Kershaw, Richland,
    Sumter

Average Flow: 6,389 feet per second or 172
    million gallons per hour at U.S. 1-601 bridge

Flood Stage: 23 feet at U.S. 1-601 (Camden)

Gradient: 60 feet or 0.8 feet per mile

Difficulty: Flatwater

Hazards: A few snags, some shallows when water
    is low

Runnable Water Level: Runnable year-round

Suitable For: Beginners accompanied by
    intermediates

Sparkleberry Swamp

Lying east of the Santee River and the northern part of Lake Marion is the 16,000-acre Sparkleberry Swamp. The bottomland hardwood swamp consists of a labyrinth of bald cypress trees and open lagoons. It's a day-trip paddling destination; the swamp has very little high ground when the Santee is up. The swamp is owned by the Santee Cooper utility company, which manages it as a natural area.

Access the swamp from the east side at Sparkleberry Landing off S-51 in Sumter County, about a mile south of the S-808 intersection and about two miles north of the Clarendon County line.

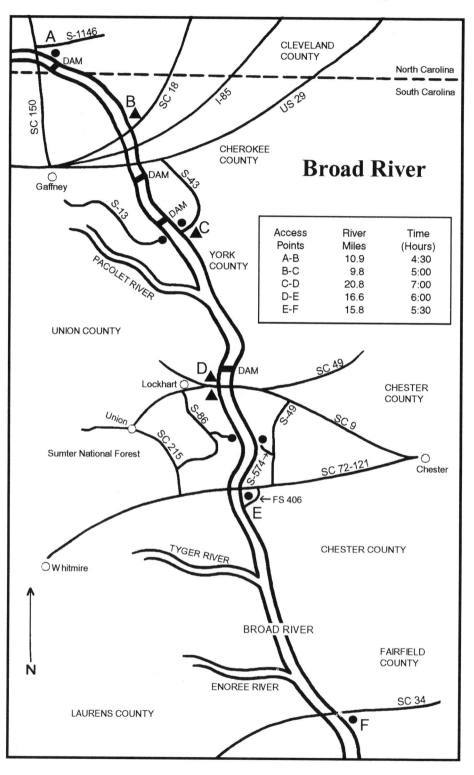

Broad River

Access Points	River Miles	Time (Hours)
A-B	10.9	4:30
B-C	9.8	5:00
C-D	20.8	7:00
D-E	16.6	6:00
E-F	15.8	5:30

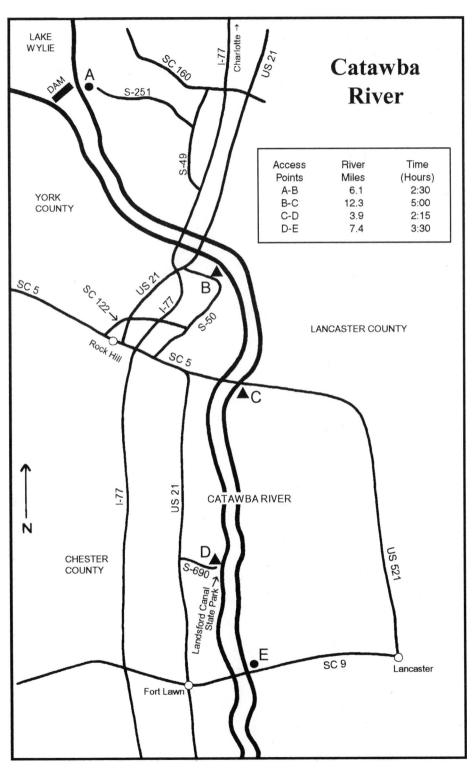

Catawba River

Access Points	River Miles	Time (Hours)
A-B	6.1	2:30
B-C	12.3	5:00
C-D	3.9	2:15
D-E	7.4	3:30

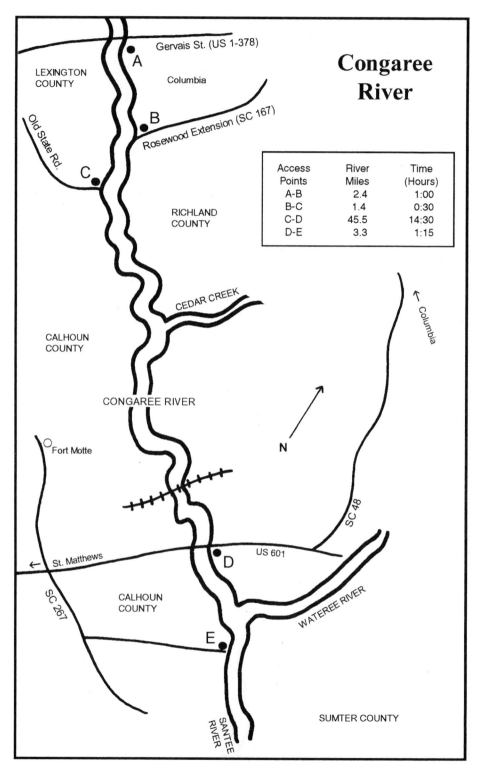

Congaree River

Access Points	River Miles	Time (Hours)
A-B	2.4	1:00
B-C	1.4	0:30
C-D	45.5	14:30
D-E	3.3	1:15

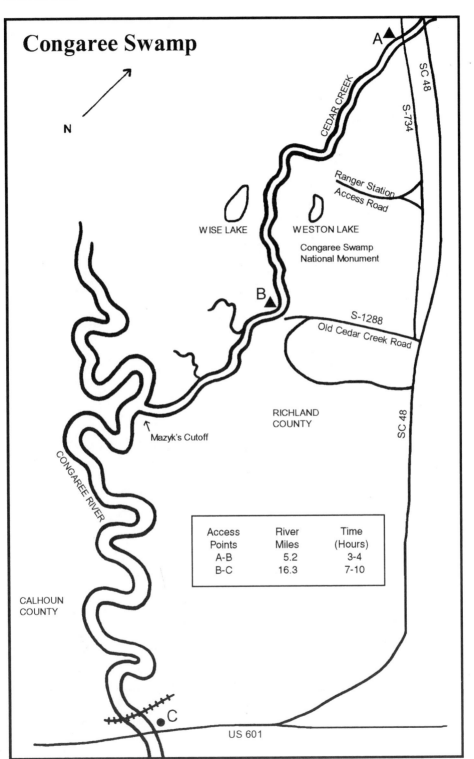

Congaree Swamp

N

A▲

CEDAR CREEK

SC 48

S-734

Ranger Station
Access Road

WISE LAKE

WESTON LAKE

Congaree Swamp
National Monument

B▲

S-1288
Old Cedar Creek Road

RICHLAND
COUNTY

SC 48

Mazyk's Cutoff

CONGAREE RIVER

CALHOUN
COUNTY

Access Points	River Miles	Time (Hours)
A-B	5.2	3-4
B-C	16.3	7-10

C

US 601

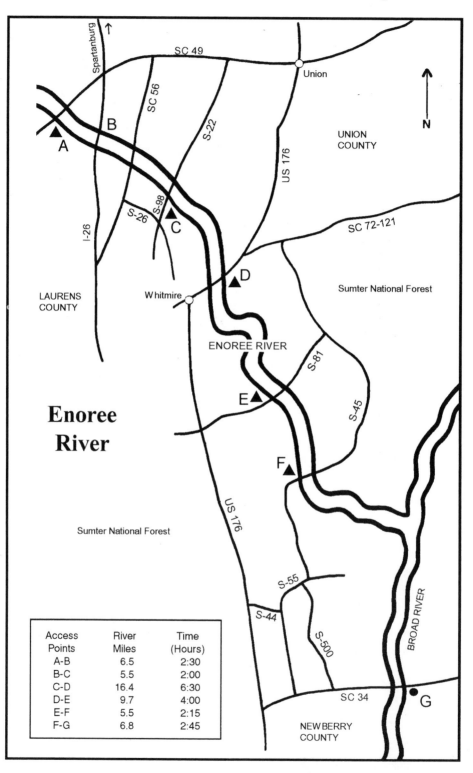

Enoree River

Access Points	River Miles	Time (Hours)
A-B	6.5	2:30
B-C	5.5	2:00
C-D	16.4	6:30
D-E	9.7	4:00
E-F	5.5	2:15
F-G	6.8	2:45

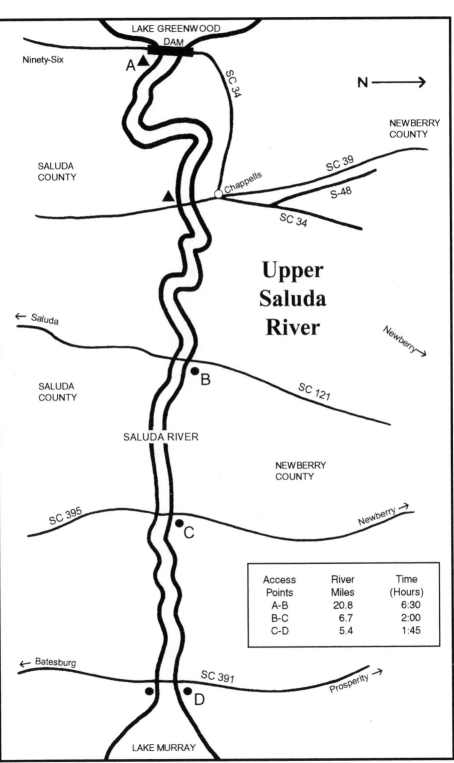

LAKE GREENWOOD DAM

Ninety-Six

A

SC 34

N

NEWBERRY COUNTY

SALUDA COUNTY

SC 39

Chappells

S-48

SC 34

Upper Saluda River

Newberry →

← Saluda

SALUDA COUNTY

B

SC 121

SALUDA RIVER

NEWBERRY COUNTY

SC 395

Newberry →

C

Access Points	River Miles	Time (Hours)
A-B	20.8	6:30
B-C	6.7	2:00
C-D	5.4	1:45

← Batesburg

SC 391

Prosperity →

D

LAKE MURRAY

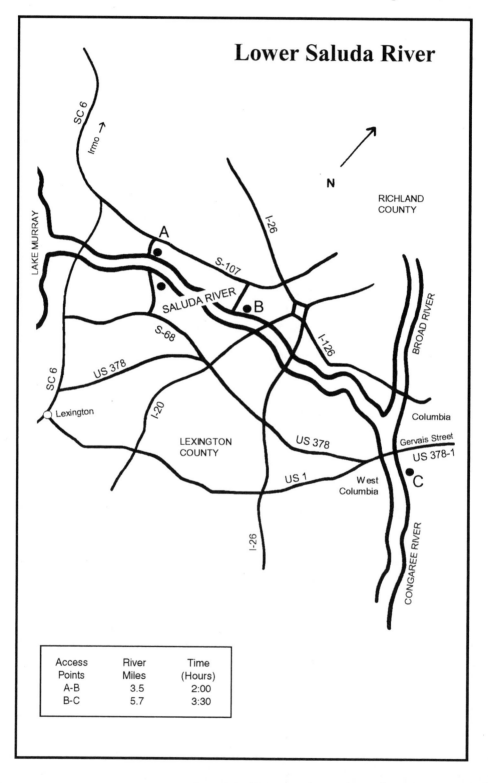

Lower Saluda River

Access Points	River Miles	Time (Hours)
A-B	3.5	2:00
B-C	5.7	3:30

Saluda River Rapids

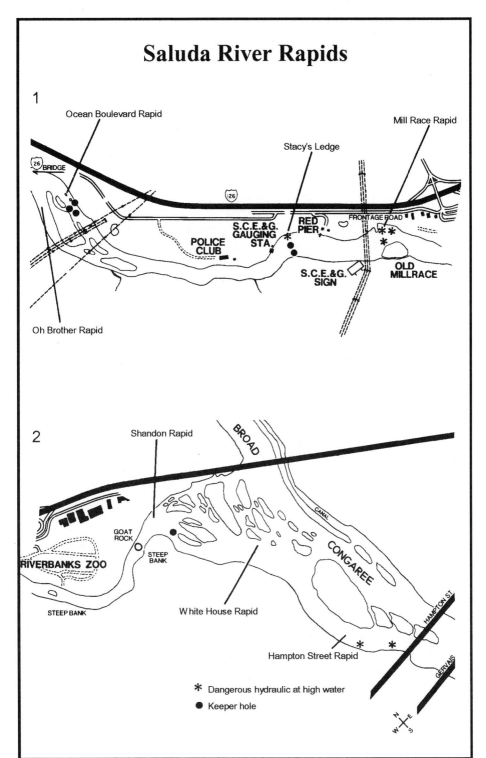

1

Ocean Boulevard Rapid

Mill Race Rapid

Stacy's Ledge

26 BRIDGE

26

RED PIER

S.C.E.&G. GAUGING STA.

FRONTAGE ROAD

POLICE CLUB

S.C.E.&G. SIGN

OLD MILLRACE

Oh Brother Rapid

2

Shandon Rapid

BROAD

GOAT ROCK

CANAL

RIVERBANKS ZOO

STEEP BANK

CONGAREE

STEEP BANK

White House Rapid

HAMPTON ST.

Hampton Street Rapid

GERVAIS

✳ Dangerous hydraulic at high water

● Keeper hole

N E W S

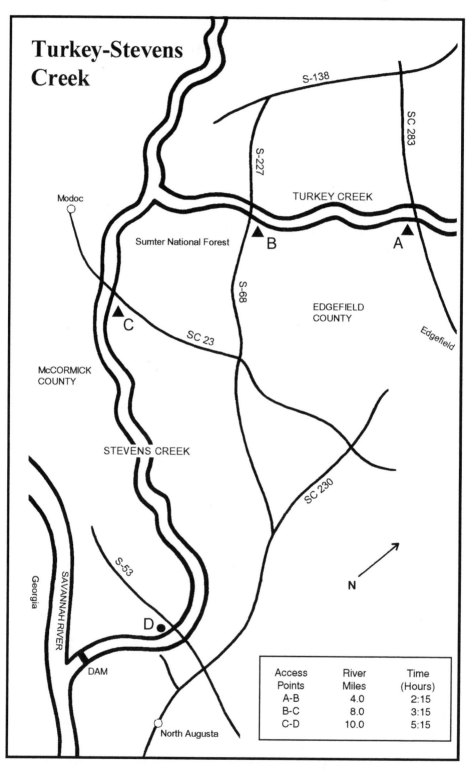

Turkey-Stevens Creek

S-138

SC 283

S-227

Modoc

TURKEY CREEK

Sumter National Forest

B

A

S-68

EDGEFIELD COUNTY

Edgefield

C

SC 23

McCORMICK COUNTY

STEVENS CREEK

SC 230

N

Georgia

SAVANNAH RIVER

S-53

S-53

D

DAM

North Augusta

Access Points	River Miles	Time (Hours)
A-B	4.0	2:15
B-C	8.0	3:15
C-D	10.0	5:15

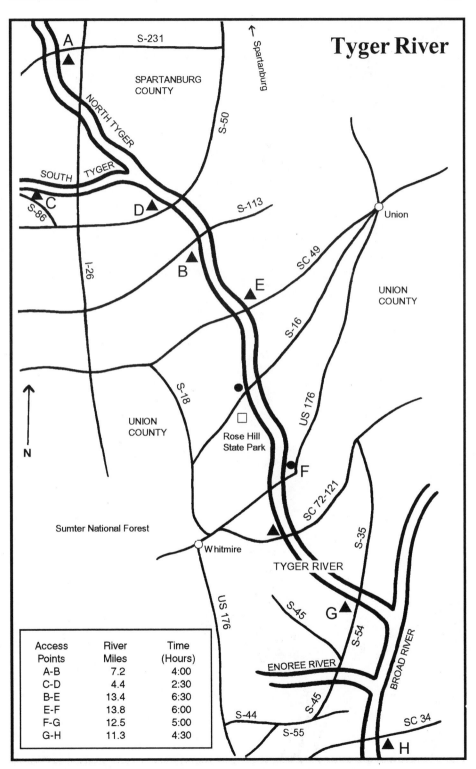

Tyger River

Access Points	River Miles	Time (Hours)
A-B	7.2	4:00
C-D	4.4	2:30
B-E	13.4	6:30
E-F	13.8	6:00
F-G	12.5	5:00
G-H	11.3	4:30

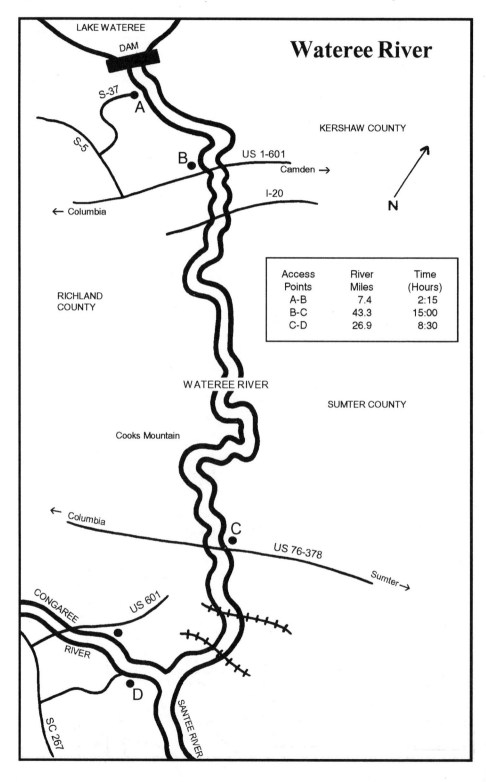

LAKE WATEREE

DAM

Wateree River

S-37

A

KERSHAW COUNTY

S-5

B

US 1-601

Camden →

I-20

← Columbia

N

RICHLAND
COUNTY

Access Points	River Miles	Time (Hours)
A-B	7.4	2:15
B-C	43.3	15:00
C-D	26.9	8:30

WATEREE RIVER

SUMTER COUNTY

Cooks Mountain

← Columbia

C

US 76-378

Sumter →

CONGAREE

US 601

RIVER

D

SANTEE RIVER

SC 267

Mountain Rivers

Chattooga
Chauga

Second Ledge on the Chattooga River tests paddlers' skills.

Chattooga River

The Chattooga River plunges into northwestern South Carolina in a frenzied, frothy rampage over massive boulders and through deep gorges of the Blue Ridge Mountains. The clear water drops nearly 2,500 feet in its 50-mile-long race from North Carolina to the backwaters of Tugaloo Lake, forming whitewater that ranges from bouncy Class I riffles to chaotic Class IV–VI waterfalls. The heart-pounding rapids combine with rugged mountain beauty to make the Chattooga the most popular whitewater river in South Carolina and one of the most paddled in the eastern United States.

Each year some 85,000 canoeists, kayakers, and rafters test their skills against the river's raw energy, challenging rapids like Bull Sluice, Eye of the Needle, and Sock Em Dog.

In 1974, the Chattooga was designated a national Wild and Scenic River with a quarter-mile-wide protective corridor. Bordering the river are the Sumter National Forest on the South Carolina side, the Chattahoochee National Forest on the Georgia side, and the Nantahala National Forest in North Carolina.

The Chattooga was relatively unknown beyond the region until 1972, when the movie *Deliverance* vaulted the river into national prominence. The movie, filmed on parts of the river, was based on the book by late South Carolina writer James Dickey. The *Deliverance* river began to attract more people—and tragedy. Between 1970 and 1975, before the U.S. Forest Service imposed safety regulations, 18 people died. Another 21 died on the river through mid-2005. Not all were boaters; some were swimmers or hikers.

Regulations require each float party leader to register. All floaters on Sections III and IV must wear a Coast Guard-approved life jacket, and those on Sections I and II must have a life jacket available. All floaters in decked craft and all those who paddle below Woodall Shoals must wear a helmet.

The Forest Service bans boating above S.C. 28. The agency is considering whether to allow canoes and kayaks on the upper 15 miles; a decision is expected by 2007.

The Chattooga is split into four sections from the upper to the lower parts of the river. Sections I and II contain fairly easy whitewater. Section III contains difficult whitewater that should be attempted only by experienced boaters. Section IV should be attempted by highly experienced boaters. If either of the latter two sections proved too difficult, boaters should walk out along the trails rather than risk injury or loss of life.

Overflow Creek Bridge to S.C. 28

This is the West Fork of the Chattooga, known as Section I. The West Fork merges with the main stem of the Chattooga just below S.C. 28 bridge, Russell Bridge, a short paddle upstream.

Put in at Overflow Creek Bridge, which is on Forest Service Road 86 (A) or at the parking lot 0.2 miles downstream (B).

This 4.0-mile run is suitable for beginners and serves as a good training stream. While the West Fork is a slow-moving mountain stream, it has two sets of Class II rapids, both of which can easily be avoided if desired.

The first occurs at Dam Sluice, a spot where loggers once built a rock jetty three-fourths of the way across the stream to create a sluice to help flush logs downstream. This sluice has a bit of a zig-zag in its and can cause a canoe to ram a boulder guarding the left bank if a proper right rudder stroke is not executed at the right time. The sluice may rate as a Class III at high water. To avoid it, paddle to the jetty and pull out.

The second set of Class II rapids comes just before the West Fork merges with the river. Called Big Slide, the rapids form where the stream cascades over a canted, flat boulder.

To complete the section, either turn upstream at the Chattooga and paddle about 350 yards to the S.C. 28 bridge (C) or float downstream 1.2 miles to the Forest Service parking lot (D) off S.C. 28.

At the S.C. 28 bridge, take out on the left (west) side below the bridge facing upstream. A parking lot is on the Georgia side of the bridge.

S.C. 28 to Earl's Ford

This is Section II. Because the Forest Service doesn't permit boating above the S.C. 28 bridge, this is a frequent starting point for many paddlers. Register at the self-registration station. The river is a little more riffly on this 6.9-mile stretch. It has a Class III rapid but nonetheless is safe enough for novice paddlers and tubers, though capsizes may be frequent.

The river flows over small shelf-like rapids and spreads out in some parts so that a walk or two may be mandatory in low water.

An alternative put-in is at the Forest Service parking lot (D). Below the parking lot, several houses on private land appear along the left bank. This is the only development other than bridges along the river's entire course.

The first significant rapid is Turn Hole, rated Class II, about 3.5 miles downstream. Move to the left to go over the main drop, then cut to the right to avoid being pushed into the bank.

Several hundred yards farther is the only Class III rapid, Big Shoals, recognizable by large rocks lined across the river. This rapid is worth scouting even in low water because of the sharp drop.

Go through on the right side, following a chute that breaks back to the left. At higher water levels, Big Shoals can be run through the center and left sides.

Earl's Ford (E) marks the end of Section II. To identify it, look for a sandy beach on the left and Warwoman Creek entering from the right.

Earl's Ford to U.S. 76

The Chattooga's famous whitewater begins in earnest at Earl's Ford, the entry point for Section III. This section takes most of a day to run. From here, the river falls 340 feet in 11.6 miles for an average drop of 29 feet per mile.

From U.S. 76, take S-196 north 6.1 miles to the four-way stop sign at S-193, turn left (west) and follow S-193 4.0 miles to the Forest Service parking lot. A 500-yard portage leads to the river.

An alternate put-in that cuts 3.0 miles off Section III is the access at Sandy Ford (F). Follow S-193 for 2.9 miles from the S-196 junction. Turn left at Forest Service Road 721-A and follow it to the parking lot.

Putting in at Sandy Ford cuts out two major rapids: Warwoman and Dick's Creek Ledge.

Warwoman Rapid, a Class II–III, is just after the first bend below Earl's Ford. Start on the left and move to the right, then turn to the left.

Dick's Creek Ledge, also called First Ledge, is nearly 2.0 miles downriver. A 60-foot-high waterfall on the right bank makes this Class IV rapid a breathtaking sight. To run the rapid, maneuver to the left center and point the boat to the right as you go over the first drop with a hard right draw to prevent being swept to the left over a rock ledge. At the bottom of the second drop, draw to the left, completing an "S" turn.

Below Dick's Creek Ledge are islands and a series of Class III drops known as Stairsteps Rapids.

The second bend below Sandy Ford is the entrance to The Narrows, a 200-yard-long gorge that is nearly impossible to portage. The Forest Service rates this constricted passage, a series of boiling water and crosscurrents, a Class IV. Scout on the left bank above the large rocks that form the entrance. Enter to the left and make an "S" turn after the first drop, back to right of center to avoid an undercut rock in the center. Below the second drop are other undercut rocks that could trap a swimmer.

Around the next bend is a guaranteed thrill, a 6-foot waterfall signaled by a pounding roar and the seeming disappearance of the river. This is Second Ledge, a

Class III. The best way to run Second Ledge is straight ahead near the left bank. The waterfall spills into a foaming pool that's big enough to safely cushion a plunging canoe.

About 1.4 miles downstream is Eye of the Needle, another Class III. It is recognizable by a large boulder protruding across most of the river from the right, leaving the "eye" on the extreme left as the only passage. A large eddy and a sandy beach on the right side below the rapid makes Eye of the Needle a popular lunch spot and observation point for watching kayakers do pop-ups.

The river flows through about 4.0 miles of smaller rapids and ledges until the next major rapid, Roller Coaster, a rollicking ride through large waves of Class II to Class III difficulty.

Painted Rock, or Keyhole, a Class III to IV, is next as the river bends to the right. Move to the left bank to scout. There are two routes here. Enter from the right of center and cut to the right to avoid a large boulder in the middle of the river. Or, from the left, drop through the rapids by moving to the right to get around the boulder.

photo by Brian Gomsak

Kayaker challenges Bull Sluice on the Chattooga River.

After Painted Rock, the Chattooga descends through smaller rapids for the next 3.0 miles, a kind of lull before the fury of Bull Sluice.

There's no mistaking Bull Sluice. Its thunderous roar echoes several hundred yards upstream. Pull over to the right when large boulders become visible on the Georgia (right) side of the river to scout or portage. Bull Sluice, a Class V, is the most dangerous rapid on Section III. By mid-2001, ten persons had lost their lives in the rapid and its keeper hydraulics, some on inner tubes before they were outlawed below Earl's Ford.

The formation of huge rocks at Bull Sluice is a popular gathering place. On a summer weekend, 50 to 100 people or more will be sitting on the rocks, clapping and cheering the Bull Sluicers after each run. Paddlers who take on the Bull should wear a helmet and set up a throw rope at the base of the dome rock on the Georgia side.

After leaving the Georgia side, move downstream and then across the river to the left and enter Bull Sluice along the South Carolina side. Pull into the eddy on the left. Ferry out from the top of the eddy and head straight over the first of the double drops just to the left of center of the upper hole. Going too far to the left, however, may mean a close call with "Decapitation Rock," so called for its neck-level height at the bottom of the first hydraulic. If you have punched the first hole, the current will sweep the boat to the left, helping it turn into the second drop head on.

After Bull Sluice, the U.S. 76 bridge (G) is in sight. Take out 100 yards above the bridge on the left at a path that leads to the Chattooga River Information Center or on the right under the bridge.

Float times based on the U.S. 76 bridge water-level gauge: 1.0 feet—7 hours; 2.0 feet—5 hours; 3.0 feet—4-1/2 hours. Subtract an hour for a party of kayaks only.

U.S. 76 to Tugaloo Lake

Section IV contains the most difficult rapids on the river and it is only for advanced paddlers who have good equipment. Open canoes need extra flotation since boats will frequently spill and fill with water. Most of the rapids are Class IV and Class V. Paddlers will see cascading waterfalls and steep gorges along this 7.9-mile section. The elevation falls 240 feet, an average gradient of 30 feet per mile.

The first rapid boaters will encounter is Surfing Rapid, a surfing wave for those who want to play. Run it on the right.

About 200 yards downstream is Screaming Left Turn, named for the sharp left turn needed to clear rocks on the right. At the far left, cut back to the right to go through the lower part of this Class IV along the right side.

Rock Jumble, a Class III, is next. Scout on the left bank. It's best to run it diagonally left to right.

From here, it's nearly 0.5 mile before Woodall Shoals (H), a possible take-out 1.8 miles below the bridge.

Woodall Shoals has a dangerous hydraulic that flows back upstream underneath a rock ledge. Seven persons have died here, underscoring the Class VI rating given by the Forest Service. Land at the rock ledge on the left to portage around the hydraulic, which is left of river center. Put in below the hydraulic and swing out to the center of the river for an exciting roller-coaster ride through the shoals. Another way to avoid the hydraulic is to follow the right side of the river. Ferry back upstream to circle above the hydraulic and move to the right bank.

At the bottom of the shoals, on the South Carolina (left) side, a foot trail leads 350 yards to the parking lot and Forest Service Road 757. The road leads to S-538, which intersects U.S. 76 2.7 miles east of the river.

Below Woodall Shoals the river narrows to half its width, a tip-off that Seven-Foot Falls is coming up. Park on the right and climb up on the big rock that overlooks the falls to scout. The crashing, churning water makes an awesome sight. The rocks channel most of the current over the 7-foot-high drop from right to left, sending the water smashing into a large boulder. A hard right draw is required to avoid this overhanging rock wall on the left. To run Seven-Foot Falls with a little more caution at higher water levels, move along the right side to an eddy immediately above the drop, then slide through the chute on the right.

Deliverance Rock Rapid, so named because several scenes from the movie *Deliverance* were shot here, boasts Class III–IV water. This rapid is recognized by a huge boulder on the right side blocking the river. Enter from the right, move to the left around the rock, and angle back to the right.

Next is Raven Rock, or Ravens Chute, aptly named for the sluice-like course through this Class III–IV rapid, set against the backdrop of a towering cliff. A good way to approach the rapid is to start at an eddy about 30 yards upstream on the right, cut diagonally across the river to the left to another eddy, then slide diagonally to the right.

At this point, it's nearly 2.0 miles to Calm Before the Storm, the last breather before confronting Five Falls, Section IV's dramatic finish.

The first rapid of Five Falls is Entrance Rapid, a Class IV. Run it from the left to the far right and then stop on the left bank to scout Corkscrew, a Class V.

Corkscrew is a frothing mass of whitewater and crosscurrents. Descend to the left, then veer to the right at the bottom.

Crack in the Rock follows immediately. Scout this Class IV from the right. From here, if you decide to portage, follow the right bank. Cracks in the boulders create three gaps. Pick the larger gap on the right; the crack on the left is undercut and dan-

photos by Lisa Birskovich

Kayaker descend through Screaming Left Turn (above) and Jawbone Rapid on the Chattooga River.

gerous.

Move to the left bank to scout Jawbone, the fourth of the 500-yard-long falls and among the most formidable. Begin at the center and move to the left after the first drop, then scout the rest of the rapid. Cut back to the center, keeping to the right of "Hydroelectric Rock," a large boulder at the bottom. The rock has a hole with water flushing through it, which traps debris and could pin a swimming paddler. Set up a throw rope here.

Ferry back to the left side below Hydroelectric Rock to scout Sock Em Dog and its Class V strength.

Begin at the left and make for the right side. A rock shelf sits in the middle of the river. At the top of the falls is a mound of water called "The Launching Pad." A run at center or just right of center helps sling-shot boats to the pool below. The pool contains rocks and a strong hydraulic, which can be a keeper at water levels higher than 1.5 feet on the U.S. 76 gauge.

The last rapid of any size before the river yields to Tugaloo Lake is Shoulder Bone, a Class III that will seem mild in comparison with the battering force of Five Falls. Enter Shoulder Bone at the left and go to the right around the extended point.

The Tugaloo Lake Road access (I) is 2.0 miles away on the left (east) bank. To reach it from U.S. 76, turn right (south) on S-538 2.7 miles east of the river, go 2.4 miles to S-102, turn right (west) at the intersection and follow S-102 for 2.9 miles to S-96, which leads to the Tugaloo Lake Road.

Average float times for Section IV based on the U.S. 76 gauge: 1.0 feet—8 hours; 1.5 feet—7 hours; 2.0 feet—5-1/2 hours. Subtract an hour for kayaks.

Chattooga River at a Glance

Trail: Overflow Creek to Tugaloo Lake Road

Length: 30.4 miles

Topographic Maps: Rainy Mountain, Satolah
      (GA), Whetstone

County Maps: Oconee, Rabun Bald (GA)

Average Flow: 658 cubic feet per second or 17.7
      million gallons per hour at U.S. 76 bridge

Flood Stage: Not established

Gradient: 680 feet or 22.4 feet per mile

Difficulty: Class II on Section I, Classes I-III on
      Section II, Classes I-V on Section III,
      Classes I-V on Section IV

Hazards: Dangerous rapids, undercut rocks,

powerful hydraulics

Runnable Water Level: Above 2.0 feet on the U.S.
76 gauge is considered dangerous; 1.5 to
2.0 feet is the optimum level; below 1.5 feet
paddlers may have to pull over rocks.

Suitable For: Sections I and II for beginner,
Section III for intermediate and advanced,
Section IV for advanced and expert

Chauga River

The Chauga, sometimes called a miniature Chattooga, cascades through the green creases of mountainous Oconee County. The narrow river bordered by hemlocks and rhododendron, contains Class III–V rapids as it drops more than 700 feet over 24 miles on its way to Lake Hartwell. The strongest rapids occur in the 400-foot-deep Chauga gorge, marked by steep walls, chutes, and drops.

The U. S. Forest Service in 2001 concluded 16.0 miles of the Chauga are eligible for National Wild and Scenic River designation. Any such recommendation to Congress would come in Fall 2002.

The agency does not encourage boating on the Chauga, 7.0 miles west of the Chattooga.

The Chauga can be divided into four sections. Section I is a 5.4-mile run between S-193 (Blackwell Bridge) and S-290 (Cassidy Bridge). Section II, the Chauga gorge, spans 9.8 miles to Cobbs Bridge. Section III is a 7.4-mile float to S-34 (Horseshoe Bridge). Section IV is 2.0 miles of flatwater that ends at Davis Bridge.

The Chauga gorge can be the most hazardous part of the river and should be paddled only by advanced canoeists and kayakers. Paddlers should take helmets, throw ropes, and extra flotation. The trip takes 8 hours. There are no accesses beyond the first 2.0 miles.

The Chauga is an unpredictable runoff river. Local canoeists paddle it when it fills after a rain. Most of the time the upper sections are too low to run. To determine water levels, check the gauge at Cassidy Bridge. Experienced Chauga paddlers say the best run is from about 4 to 12 inches above zero. Above 12 inches the river gets too dangerous to run. Other guidebooks list 6 inches above zero as the maximum level.

S-193 to S290

At the beginning of Section I, the Chauga is more like a stream than a river. Put in at the landing on the right (west) side above the bridge.

About a mile downstream is the Chauga Narrows, a 15-foot-high waterfall followed by a 100-foot-long chute formed by a sheer gorge. Portage on the right.

Just below is a smaller chute, a Class IV because of the undercut rock on the left.

The rest of the section is a series of Class II and Class III drops and ledges. Take out at the landing on the right (west) side above the bridge.

S-290 to Cobbs Bridge

Section II, the Chauga gorge, drops 415 feet or 42 feet per mile. Get an early start, this is an all-day trip.

After a half mile of flatwater, the first waterfall appears. A 100-foot-long chute breaks to the right into a pool. Portage on the right.

Several hundred yards below, the river constricts into a drop to the left. Warning: Eddy out in the pool to the left. A strong current could wash unwary paddlers over a 15-foot-high waterfall called Super Sock-Em-Dog. Portage on the left if unrunnable.

Nearly 2.0 miles of large rapids follow. The first is a Class III-IV chute. Enter from the right, then cut back to the left to ride the slanted chute.

Two pools later is Class III-IV. Move to the left and punch through the center of the rapid.

About 20 minutes later is Staircase, a Class IV-V that follows a chute along the left bank and cuts under an overhanging rock.

The last major rapid is a Class III chute that makes a right-angle turn to the left.

Riley Moore Falls, which spans the river, is about 2.0 miles above Cobbs Bridge. Portage on the right to get around this 15-foot waterfall.

Cobbs Bridge has no public access. Arrange with the property owners at the bridge for a put-in or take-out.

Cobbs Bridge to S-34

This 4-hour float is the Chauga's most popular run.

About 2.0 miles downstream is a large rock formation with a Class II chute that breaks from left to right.

Below U.S. 76, at the Chau Ram County Park, Pumphouse Rapid has a Class III chute on the left and a drop on the right.

Almost 150 yards below the foot bridge is Can Opener, so named because an undercut rock can slice open a canoe hull. Hit right of center to avoid a submerged rock in this Class II-III.

Take out at a throw-in on the right (west) side below Horseshoe Bridge (S-34).

S-34 to Davis Bridge

The Chauga is a flatwater stream meandering past farms and houses for its last 2.0 miles to Davis Bridge. Take out on either side.

Chauga River at a Glance

Trail: S-293 to Davis Bridge

Length: 24.6 miles

Topographic Maps: Holly Springs, Whetstone

County Maps: Oconee

Average Flow: Not available

Flood Stage: Not established

Gradient: 772 feet or 31.4 feet per mile

Difficulty: Class I, II, III, IV, and V rapids

Hazards: Logs, waterfalls, undercut rocks, keeper
    hydraulics, and lack of access in the Chauga
    Gorge

Runnable Water Level: May be too low to run in
    dry seasons

Suitable For: Section I for intermediate, Section II
    for advanced, Section III for intermediate,
    Section IV for beginner

photo by Jack Horan

Inflatable kayak slides into Chauga River's Can Opener Rapid.

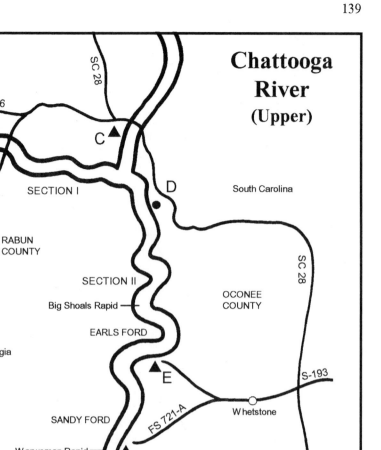

Chattooga River (Upper)

SC 28

FS 86

A

B

C

D

SECTION I

South Carolina

RABUN COUNTY

GA 884

SECTION II

Big Shoals Rapid

EARLS FORD

Georgia

OCONEE COUNTY

SC 28

E

S-193

SANDY FORD

FS 721-A

Whetstone

Warwoman Rapid

F

Dicks Creek Ledge

Sumter National Forest

N

SECTION III

The Narrows Rapid

S-196

Chattahoochee National Forest

Second Ledge

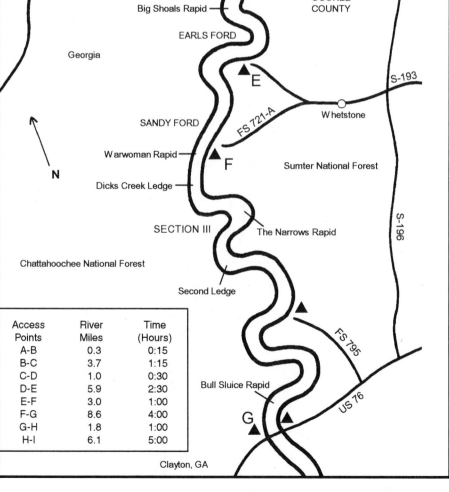

FS 795

Bull Sluice Rapid

US 76

G

Access Points	River Miles	Time (Hours)
A-B	0.3	0:15
B-C	3.7	1:15
C-D	1.0	0:30
D-E	5.9	2:30
E-F	3.0	1:00
F-G	8.6	4:00
G-H	1.8	1:00
H-I	6.1	5:00

Clayton, GA

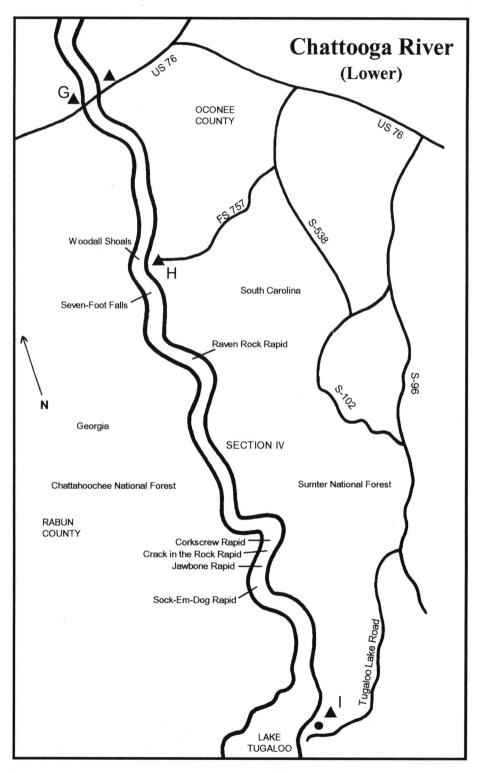

Chattooga River Rapids

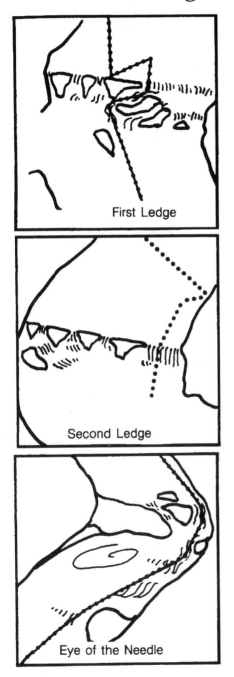

First Ledge

Second Ledge

Eye of the Needle

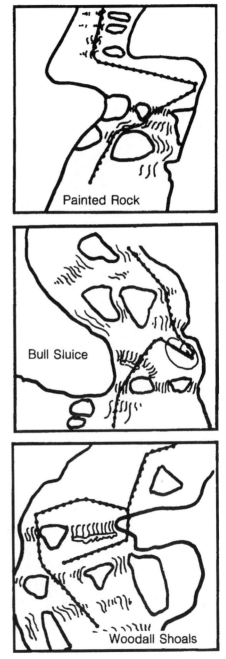

Painted Rock

Bull Sluice

Woodall Shoals

Chattooga River Rapids

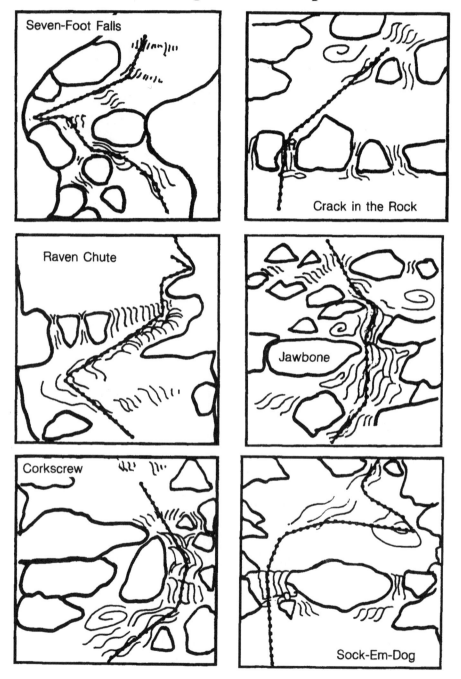

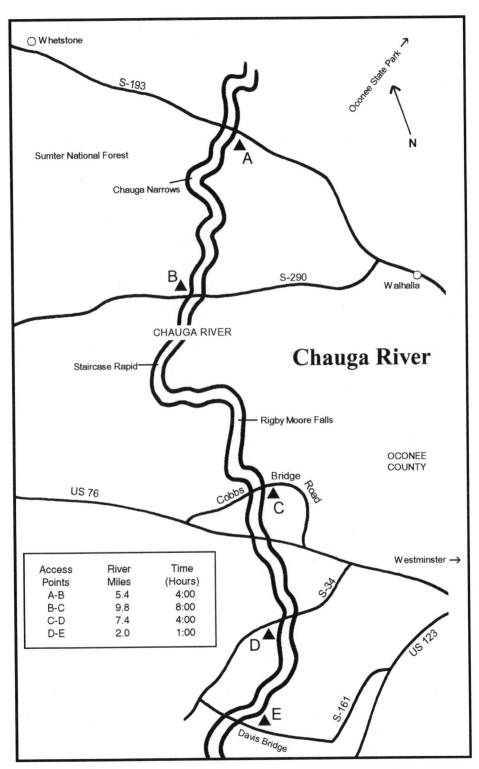

Other Major Rivers

This section lists landmarks and landings as well as mileages for other large South Carolina rivers and river segments not covered in the river trail descriptions. These rivers are paddled less often by canoeists and kayakers because of wide expanses of open water, tides, or dams. Listed in the following summaries are the lower Broad, the Cooper, the Coosawhatchie-Broad, the Great Pee Dee, the Savannah, and the lower Waccamaw.

Broad River (Lower)

The Broad starts in the foothills of North Carolina and passes through the Piedmont of South Carolina before merging with the Saluda at Columbia to form the Congaree. This section picks up just below the end of the Broad River trail.

> Beginning of Section: Parr Shoals Dam
> End of Section: Saluda River confluence
> Length: 24.7 miles
> Topographic Maps: Blair, Columbia-North, Irmo,
> Pomario, Richtex
> County Maps: Fairfield, Newberry, Richland

Mileage Points	Miles
Parr Shoals Dam	0.0
To. S.C. 213	0.8
To Bookman Island	13.1
To Diversion Dam	9.9
To Middle Creek Landing	4.0
To Saluda River confluence	0.4

Cooper River

The Cooper River flows from Lake Moultrie through the Pinopolis Dam in Berkeley County and travels through an industrialized area of North Charleston before meeting the Ashley River at Charleston.

Beginning of Section: Pinopolis Dam

End of Section: Ashley River confluence

Length: 48.1 miles

Topographic Maps: Charleston, Cordesville,
       Kittredge, North Charleston

County Maps: Berkeley, Charleston

Mileage Points	Miles
Pinopolis Dam	0.0
To U.S. 52	2.3
To Strawberry Landing	11.3
To Moreland landing	12.9
To U.S. 17	24.0
To Ashley River confluence	1.4

Coosawhatchie-Broad Rivers

The Coosawhatchie flows through Hampton and Jasper Counties before joining the Broad River in Beaufort County. The Broad is joined by the Chechessee River at Port Royal Sound.

Beginning of Section: S-87

End of Section: Chechessee River confluence

Length: 36.8 miles

Topographic Maps: Laurel Bay, Parris Island,
       Spring Island, Yemassee

County Maps: Beaufort, Jasper

Mileage Points	Miles
S-87	0.0
To U.S. 17	10.3
To I-95	0.3
To Broad River confluence	8.1
To Railroad	1.1
To S.C. 170	10.1
To Chechessee River confluence	6.9

Great Pee Dee River

The Great Pee Dee River courses through the east-central part of the state, draining both the Little Pee Dee and Lynches Rivers before spilling into Winyah Bay at Georgetown.

Beginning of Section: South Carolina state line
End of Section: Winyah Bay
Length: 171.0 miles
Topographic Maps: Cheraw, Drake, Florence-
    East, Georgetown-North, Georgetown-South,
    Hyman, Johnsonville, Mont Clare, Morven-
    East, Oak Grove, Outland, Plantersville,
    Society Hill, Wallace, Waverly Mills,
    Witherspoon Island, Yauhannah
County Maps: Chesterfield, Darlington, Dillon,
    Florence, Georgetown, Horry, Marion,
    Marlboro, Williamsburg

Mileage Points	Miles
South Carolina line	0.0
To U.S. 1	8.2
To U.S. 15-401	16.5
To Plumfield Landing	2.3
To Witherspoon Island	17.7
To I-95	6.3
To U.S. 76-301	11.1
To Carter Landing	3.8
To Catfish Landing	18.0
To U.S. 378	7.6
To Port Hill Landing	15.4
To Little Pee Dee confluence	20.8
To U.S. 701	4.9
To Lower Topsaw Landing	4.8
To U.S. 17	23.0
To Winyah Bay	0.6

Savannah River

The largest and longest river in the state, the Savannah forms the boundary between South Carolina and Georgia. The upper part of the Savannah consists of a series of dammed lakes with little free-flowing water. The river's remaining free-flowing section begins at the Stevens Creek dam, just above Augusta, Ga., and ends at the Atlantic Ocean.

Beginning of Section: Stevens Creek Dam

End of Section: U.S. 17A

Length: 189.9 miles

Topographic Maps: Augusta-East (GA), Blue
   Springs Landing (GA), Brier Creek Landing,
   Brighton, Burtons Ferry (GA), Girard, Girard-
   Northwest, Hardeeville, Jackson, Kildare,
   Limehouse, Martinez (GA), Mechanic Hill,
   Millett, North Augusta, Pineland, Port
   Wentworth, Rincon, Savannah (GA), Shell
   Bluff (GA)

County Maps: Aiken, Allendale, Barnwell, Burke
   (GA), Chatham (GA), Columbia (GA),
   Edgefield, Effingham (GA), Hampton, Jasper,
   Richmond (GA), Screven (GA)

Mileage Points	Miles
Stevens Creek Dam	0.0
To I-20	3.0
To North Augusta Landing	3.0
To U.S. 1-78-378	2.4
To S.C.-GA. 283	0.6
To New Savannah Bluff Lock and Dam	8.4
To Richmond County Landing (GA)	0.5
To Silver Bluff Landing	12.3
To Shell Bluff Landing (GA)	10.9
To Handcock Landing (GA)	9.1
To Brigham's Landing (GA)	8.1
To Stoney Bluff Landing (GA)	10.9
To Johnson's Landing	8.6

To U.S. 301-Burton's Ferry Landing (GA)	5.6
To Cohen's Bluff Landing	14.8
To Blue Springs Landing (GA)	25.7
To S.C.-GA. 119	16.7
To Ebenezer Landing (GA)	16.7
To Millstone Landing	10.8
To I-95	5.8
To U.S. 17	6.6
To U.S. 17A	6.4

Waccamaw River (Lower)

The Waccamaw River originates in North Carolina and flows through Horry and Georgetown Counties before emptying into Winyah Bay at Georgetown. This section picks up at the end of the Waccamaw River trail.

Beginning of Section: U.S. 501 Bypass

End of Section: Winyah Bay

Length: 48.8 miles

Topographic Maps: Brookgreen Gardens, Bucksville, Conway, Georgetown-South, Waverly Mills

County Maps: Georgetown, Horry

Mileage Points	Miles
U.S. 501 Bypass	0.0
To Peachtree Landing	16.5
To Wacca Wache Landing	13.5
To Butler Island	12.0
To U.S. 17	5.4
To Winyah Bay	0.6

Part III

Paddling group beaches canoes on the Santee River.

photo by Jack Horan

Appendix A

Listed are state and federal agencies and private groups that can provide helpful information on paddling South Carolina's rivers.

South Carolina Department of Natural Resources

The S.C. Department of Natural Resources, among its other functions, oversees boating, fishing, and hunting laws and the state's scenic rivers program. The mailing address for the main office is P.O. Box 167, Columbia, S.C. 29202. The department's Web address is www.dnr.state.sc.us. The Web site for the state trails program is www.sctrails.net/Trails.

S.C. Department of Natural Resources Law Enforcement Offices

Region I
Clemson Office
153 Hopewell Road
Pendleton, SC 29670
(864) 654-8255, ext. 18
FAX (864) 624-9158

Region II
Florence Office
2007 Pisgah Road
Florence, SC 29501
(803) 661-4766
FAX (803) 661-4717

Region III
Columbia Office
PO Box 167
1000 Assembly Street
(803) 734-4303
FAX (803) 734-3962

Region IV
Ft. Johnson Office
PO Box 12559
217 Ft. Johnson Road
Charleston, SC 29412
(843) 953-9307
FAX (843) 953-9321

ACE Basin Project
Donnelley Wildlife Management Area
585 Donnelley Drive
Green Pond, SC 29446
(843) 844-8957

South Carolina State Park Service
1205 Pendleton Street
Columbia, SC 29201
(830) 734-0193
www.southcarolinaparks.com

Catawba River Dams Relicensing

Paddlers can expect to see improved timing for releases of water from the Lake Wylie, Lake Wateree, and Fishing Creek dams on the Catawba River by 2008

That's because Duke Power Company, to win new 50-year federal licenses for the dams, must provide for recreation and wildlife on free-flowing sections of the river below the dams.

In 2004, Duke proposed minimal, round-the-clock flows from the Wylie and Wateree dams to benefit fish and other aquatic life. There are no guaranteed flows now—they are unpredictable, based on electricity demand. The utility also proposed recreational releases, higher in volume, from the Wylie dams for warm-weather holidays plus each Friday, Saturday, and Sunday from May through September, as well as the last weekend in April and first weekend in October. Releases from the Wateree dam would be identical except there would be no Friday releases. Thus, canoeists and kayakers could launch on those days knowing they'll have enough water.

Additionally, the Great Falls area, 40 miles north of Columbia, may get scheduled whitewater paddling. Duke has proposed six days of releases a year for Class II–IV rapids in two bypassed channels; American Whitewater, an advocacy group, has proposed 28 days of releases. Before Duke, in 1907, diverted the water for electricity generation, the section of was called "The Great Falls of the Catawba" for its booming cataracts.

Rocky shoals spider lilies bloom from mid-May to early June on the Catawba River at Landsford Canal State Park.

Francis Marion and Sumter National Forests

The U.S. Forest Service manages the Francis Marion and Sumter National Forests. The Broad River, Chattooga River, Chauga River, Enoree River, Santee River, Turkey-Stevens Creeks, Tyger River, and Wambaw Creek fully or in part flow through these national forests.

U.S. Forest Service
Supervisor's Office
4931 Broad River Road
Columbia, SC 29210-4021
(803) 561-4000
www.fs.fed.us/r8/fms

Francis Marion National Forest

Wambaw Office
1015 Pinckney Street
McClellanville, SC 29458
(843) 887-3257

Witherbee Office
2421 Witherbee Road
Cordesville, SC 29434
(843) 336-3248

Sumter National Forest

Enoree Ranger District
Enoree Office
20 Work Center Road
Whitmire, SC 29178
(803) 276-4810

Enoree Ranger District
Tyger Office
3557 Whitmire Highway
Union, SC 29379
(864) 427-9858

Long Cane Ranger District
810 Buncombe Street
Edgefield, SC 29824
(803) 637-5396

Andrew Pickens Ranger District
112 Andrew Pickens Circle
Mountain Rest, SC 29664
(864) 638-9568

U.S. Geological Survey, WRD
720 Gracern Road, Suite 129
Columbia, SC 29210
(803) 750-6100
http://waterdata.usgs.gov

National Weather Service
Weather Forecast Office Columbia
2909 Aviation Way
West Columbia, SC 29170-2102
(803) 822-8135
www.nws.noaa.gov

Flood Stages

Here are flood stages used by the National Weather Service in South Carolina.

River	Flood Stage	Location
Black	12 feet	Kingstree
Broad	19 feet	Blair, near S.C. 34 bridge
Broad	10 feet	Gaffney
Congaree	115 feet	Carolina Eastman
Congaree	19 feet	Columbia
Edisto	10 feet	Givhans Ferry
Great Pee Dee	30 feet	Cheraw
Great Pee Dee	19 feet	Pee Dee
Little Pee Dee	9 feet	Galivants Ferry
Lynches	14 feet	Effingham
North Fork Edisto	8 feet	Orangeburg
Reedy	8 feet	Greenville
Saluda	14 feet	Chappells
Saluda	9 feet	West Pelzer
Santee	10 feet	Jamestown
Savannah	32 feet	Augusta (GA)
Savannah	15 feet	Burton's Ferry (GA)
Savannah	21 feet	Butler Creek
Savannah	11 feet	Clio
Stevens Creek	18 feet	Modoc
Waccamaw	7 feet	Conway
Wateree	21 feet	Camden

Guides

The Scenic Rivers Program's Favorite Canoe and Kayak Trails of South Carolina. A 27-page guide to 12 selected rivers. To obtain a copy, mail a check for $5.50 (postage included) to S.C. Department of Natural Resources, P.O. Box 167, Columbia, SC 29202-0167. Proceeds go to the Scenic Rivers Trust Fund to assist river conservation in South Carolina.

South Carolina Atlas and Gazetteer. Detailed, shaded relief maps of the state with major and minor roads, lakes and waterways, boat ramps, fishing spots, golf courses, wildife viewing areas and much more in a friendly, oversized book format. Forty-eight quad maps include a grid system to use the atlas with GPS receivers. *Gazetteer* adds tips on places to stop and activities to enjoy. It is available at *South Carolina Wildlife* magazine's Wildlife Shop at 1000 Assembly Street in Columbia. To order by mail, call (803) 734-3944 or toll-free at (888) 644-9453, or go onlne at www.scwildlife.com. It is also available at many bookstores. Current price is $19.95.

Available July 2006

South Carolina Wildlife Outdoor Guide. A county-by-county atlas including public boat landings and facilities, state parks, heritage preserves, natural areas, hospitals, fire stations, and much more. Produced and published by South Carolina Department of Natural Resources, PO Box 167, Columbia, SC 29202-0167. This guide is invaluable for those who spend time outdoors and on the road. Contact *South Carolina Wildlife* magazine's Wildlife Shop next summer for availability and information. Size: 11 x 17 inches. Tentative price: $20.

The South Carolina Professional Paddlesport Association (SCPPA) is a non-profit organization of canoe and kayak outfitters and guides. The SCPPA can be reached at 1107 State Street, Cayce, SC 29033 or online at www.paddlesc.com.

Appendix B

Canoe, Kayak Outfitters

ACE Basin Outpost
U.S. 17 at the Ashepoo River
Jacksonboro, SC
(800) 785-2925
www.southsportonline.com

Adventure Carolina
1107 State St.
Cayce, SC 29033
(803) 796-4505
www.adventurecarolina.com

Barefoot Island Sports
1160 Pleasant Pines Rd.
Mount Pleasant, SC 29464
(843) 568-3222
www.barefootislandsports.com

Beaufort Kayak Tours
2709 Oaklawn Ave.
Beaufort, SC 29902
(843) 525-0810
www.beaufortkayaktours.com

Betwixt the Rivers
Marion, SC 29571
(843) 423-1919
btxrivers@aol.com

Black River Outdoors Center &
Expeditions
21 Garden Ave., Hwy. 701 North
Georgetown, SC 29440
(843) 546-4840
www.blackriveroutdoors.com

Blackwater Adventures
P.O. Box 4639
Pinopolis, SC 29469
(800) 761-1850, (843) 761-1850
www.blackwateradventure.com

Carolina Heritage Outfitters
U.S. 15
Canadys, SC 29433
(843) 563-5051
www.canoesc.com

Coastal Expeditions
514-B Mill St.
Mount Pleasant, SC 29464
(843) 884-7684
www.coastalexpeditions.com

Cool Breeze Kayaking
Hilton Head Island, SC
(877) 286-5154
(843) 342-3699
www.hiltonheadisland.com

Edisto Island Tidal Tours
P.O. Box 164
Edisto Island, SC 29438
(843) 869-1937

The Kayak Farm LLC
1289 Sea Island Parkway
St. Helena, SC 29920
(843) 838-2008
www.beaufortonline.com/
thekayakfarm

Lowcountry Adventures Outdoors
235 Pauls Chapel St.
Ulmer, SC 29849
(803) 707-4350
www.lowcountryoutdoors.com

Middleton Outdoor Center
4290 Ashley River Road
Charleston, SC 29414
(800) 543-4474
www.middletonplace.org

Nature Adventures Outfitters
1900 Iron Swamp Road
Awendaw, SC 29429
(800) 673-0679
www.natureadventuresoutfitters.com

Ocean Air Sea Kayak
520 Folly Rd., No. 332
Charleston, SC 29412
(800) 698-8718
(843) 586-6359
www.oceanairseakayak.com

Outside Hilton Head
The Plaza at Shelter Cove, Suite H
Hilton Head Island, SC 29928
(800) 686-6996
www.outsidehiltonhead.com

Palm Key/Tullifinny Joe's
330 Coosaw Way
Ridgeland, SC 29936
(800) 228-8420
(843) 726-5030
www.palmkey.com

Swampgirls Kayak Tours
P.O. Box 554
Hardeeville, SC 29927
(843) 784-2249
(843) 301-1778
www.swampgirls.com

Tidal Trails
1739 Maybank Highway B8
Charleston, SC 29412
(843) 768-5680
TidalTrails@prodigy.net

Canoeists pause along an upland section of the Ashepoo River.

Appendix C

Bibliography

Bostick, Lucy Hampton and Fant H. Thornley. *Mills' Atlas of South Carolina*. Columbia, 1983.

Lawson, John. *A New Voyage to Carolina*. Edited by Hugh Talmadge Lefler. Chapel Hill: University of North Carolina Press, 1967.

National Park Service. *The Nationwide Rivers Inventory*. Washington, DC: National Park Service, 1982.

Neuffer, Claude and Irene Neuffer. *Correct Mispronunciations of Some South Carolina Names*. Columbia: University of South Carolina Press, 1983.

South Carolina Water Resources Commission. *A Reconnaissance Survey of Streams in the South Carolina Coastal Plain for Consideration as a Part of the National Wild and Scenic River System*. Columbia: South Carolina Water Resources Commission, 1971.

South Carolina Water Resources Commission. *South Carolina State Water Assessment*. Columbia: South Carolina Water Resources Commission, 1983.

South Carolina Wildlife Magazine, various issues (Columbia: South Carolina Department of Natural Resources)

U.S. Fish and Wildlife Service. *Significant Wildlife Resource Areas of South Carolina*. Asheville, NC: U.S. Fish and Wildlife Service, 1981.

Index

About the Authors

GENE ABLE was a writer, journalist, and teacher of college English in Georgetown, South Carolina. A native of Ridgeland in Jasper County, Able worked for *The Island Packet* on Hilton Head Island, *The State* in Columbia, the *Independent News* in Irmo, the Rock Hill *Herald*, and the *Coastal Observer* on Pawley's Island. He was the author of *Exploring South Carolina* and had paddled more than 2,500 miles on the state's rivers.

JACK HORAN, a paddler for more than thirty years, is outdoors correspondent for *The Charlotte Observer*. His 1993 newspaper series, "Vanishing Carolinas," won the Southern Environmental Law Center's first annual Phillip D. Reed Memorial Award for outstanding environmental writing. He is author of the 1997 guidebook, *Where Nature Reigns: The Wilderness Areas of the Southern Appalachians.*

photo by Brian Gomsak

Railroad trestle marks shady spot on the Lynches River.